A Mom Finds Hope in Grief and Loss

Tragedy's
Treasures

KARYN ALMENDAREZ

I dedicate this book to my beautiful daughter, Amy. I understand how Bart's death rocked your world, and how much you miss him.

I am so proud of the many ways you exhibit your faith in Christ with your husband, your children, and with me.

I love you very much,
MOM

YOUR FREE GIFT

To thank you for reading, I would like to give you a free self-care journal and keep you up to date with new releases and special offers.

Click **HERE** to get access to your free copy.
https://openyourtreasures.com/free-gift-self-care-journal/

Go **Here** To learn more about Karyn Almendarez
https://openyourtreasures.com/learn-more-about-karyn/

INTRODUCTION

"The darker the night, the brighter the stars,
The deeper the grief, the closer is God!"
—Fyodor Dostoyevsky, Crime and Punishment

A child's death is the deepest and most excruciating tragedy a parent experiences. Too many parents have lost children, and each loss is personal and unique. If you or someone you know is grieving, there is no prescription for working through the process. However, there is hope for the initial, searing pain to lessen and leave precious memories in its place.

TRAGEDY'S TREASURES, A MOM FINDS HOPE IN GRIEF AND LOSS, shares the possibilities of positives and the hope born out of tragedies. This book encourages you to cling to God as He comforts and equips you for your grief journey.

"Call upon Me in the day of trouble; I will deliver you,
and you shall glorify Me."—Psalms 50:15 (NKJV)

THE TRAGEDY

"Mrs. Granger, you need to come to the office for a phone call. There is a nurse on the phone wanting to talk to you about an accident your son has been in."

Everyone knows if the school's secretary leaves her desk to come to your classroom to deliver a message, it is a serious situation!

The lesson I was teaching on that October day in 1997 was for a Bible class. Faith versus fear was the topic as we read:

"For God has not given us a spirit of fear,
but of power and of love and of a sound mind."
—2 Timothy 1:7 NKJV

Before this interruption, I was drawing a picture on the wipe-off board at the front of our classroom. The picture was a road splitting into two paths: one labeled faith, and the other fear.

I did not know at the time, but after I left our sixth-grade classroom to answer the call in the office, a student walked quietly to the front of the room to lead his classmates in a prayer for the life-changing news I would soon hear.

That one phone call set me in motion down a grief-stricken path. To sustain me, I would need to call on every ounce of my faith in God to survive.

THE TREASURES

How often do we find treasures? Why do we find them? Where do we find them? Will one treasure lead to another?

Answers to these questions peak our interest in childhood. But, as adults the treasures may come through tragedies if we are willing to "hang tight" and stay open to them.

Sadly, too many parents have experienced the death of a child. After such a loss, we never move beyond the suffering. My intentions are not to cause you to relive pain and misery or to worry unnecessarily what the future might hold.

Instead, I want to share the possibilities of positives which can evolve from any tragedy, and to encourage you to lean on God to give you the strength you need.

This book shares my journey through grief caused by the loss of my sixteen-year-old son in an early morning car accident. I say, "early morning car accident," because to protect his legacy, it is important that you know the accident was not alcohol or drug-related.

My faith-guided journey will travel through twelve sequential treasures, each one leading to the next. For me, these treasures revealed themselves through circumstances, prayers, choices, and divine intervention.

WHAT YOU WILL LEARN

- You are NOT alone in your feelings, thoughts, and questions.

- You have the right to work through grief your way.
- You are "normal," not crazy.
- You are worthy of love and care as you honor your loved one.

PRAISE FOR Tragedy's Treasures, A Mom Finds Hope in Grief and Loss

"In this tender personal narrative, Karyn provides a much-needed insight into the painful journey of losing a child. She compassionately describes the story of a loving wife, mother, and teacher as she processes through the reality of painful loss and the redemption of love.

Her application of Scripture and honest appraisals of fear and doubt make her story a valuable resource for people who have faced the pain of losing a child as well as people who help others heal through these tragedies."

— Penny A. Armstrong, ED.D
Education Consultant and Author

"How could God expect me, an introvert, to climb out of my box of misery to share my thoughts and feelings with others?" asks author, Karyn Almendarez. I, for one, am grateful she faced her fears, saw the value in sharing (for herself and others), and found her voice.

We learn early on in her book that her son, Bart, died at 16-yrs-old in a tragic accident (although she later reflects "There Are No Accidents"). Yet she takes her time, seemingly preparing us, circling back to help us understand her life, Bart's life, who they were at that moment in time, before sharing the full impact of a young life taken and lives changed forever.

It is evident that her Christian faith and beliefs greatly influence her journey through her grief, her ability to find acceptance in what is, to feel the ultimate agony, and yet be vulnerable, and continue to be open to life.

Her story inspires trust that experiencing excruciating pain and a good life are not mutually exclusive, that indeed, there may be treasures in our tragedies. Yet her story is not Pollyanna...it is real, and at times raw; her words are succinct and poignant, and in no way gratuitous.

The book is not a "playbook" for getting through grief. It is one woman's story told after considerable reflection, sharing her heart and soul...and I believe it is indeed our stories that inspire and can bring hope and healing."

—Pam Schofield
Licensed Professional Counselor

A WORD FROM THE AUTHOR

For anyone grieving their own loss or comforting another, I pray this book comforts you and nudges you closer to acceptance, faith, peace, and hope.

Grief is ongoing and comes in waves. Through twenty-plus years, I have learned how the intensity of pain lessens, but never goes away. We never stop missing our loved one.

That ache is always present, especially on special days and holidays.

Perhaps this book will help you know what to expect and how to help others who are grieving.

I am not a minister or trained counselor. I am proud to be a wife, mother of two, grandmother (GIGI) of four, a retired teacher, and a believer in God's perfect plan.

Blessings,

Karyn Almendarez

CALLINGS AND GIFTS

"For the gifts and the calling of God are irrevocable."
— Romans 11:29 (NKJV)

Have you ever wondered why "gifts and the calling of God" are in the same sentence? What is the meaning of *irrevocable*? Why does Scripture list *gifts* first?

I once heard a minister share a story during a funeral that I will never forget. Looking at the front of a handmade hooked rug or hand-sewn tapestry, you see many colors blending into a clear picture or pattern. But if you turn it over and look at the back of the rug, you see threads of varied colors randomly crossing each other with no continuity of any picture or design.

We see the backside during our time on Earth. The different colored threads cross randomly in patterns that don't always make sense. But when we die and go to heaven, the puzzle is solved. We see the front of the rug. All the pain, sorrows, illnesses, and trials blend into perfect harmony to form a complete and beautiful picture of who God created us to be.

The best gift God gave us was in the form of His Son, Jesus. When we believe Jesus is the only acceptable sacrifice for our sins and that He died in our place, the Holy Spirit connects with our hearts and minds to assure us God is calling.

Perhaps when God calls us to do something, He leads us closer to the gifts He has always had in store for us. Then, He nudges us to move in the directions He knows are best.

Romans 11:29 also says both His gifts and His calling are "irrevocable," which means binding. Some synonyms given are irreversible, unchangeable, and permanent.

I am the first to admit I have not always heard what He is calling me to do. Even if I do "hear" it, I do not always follow it. I am sure my self-absorption and procrastination slow down or hide the gifts He has for me.

But I am thankful I heard and obeyed His call to:

- TEACH
- MOTHER
- GROW

Honestly, it has been more challenging, but not impossible, to appreciate His calling for me to:

- GRIEVE
- TRUST
- LIVE

This book is divided into five parts.

In Part One, titled THE MAP, go back in time with me to learn how the *callings* in my life prepared me for the death of my son.

In Part Two, titled THE MAZE, read the circumstances of my life-changing, tragic loss. Learn how God *called* and equipped me to survive the initial shock of grief and move forward with His plan for me to trust and live with hope.

In Part Three, titled THE PUZZLE, explore three gifts I received which sustained me, comforted me, and gave me peace.

In Part Four, titled THE LIVING, come alongside me and experience my treasures of healing, changing (for the better), and finding renewed purpose, joy, and hope.

In Part Five, titled THE STORY CONTINUES, read the stories shared by Bart's friends and teachers, of how his life and legacy continue to change lives.

CONTENTS

PART ONE: THE MAP

"When the door of opportunity of your storehouse opens for you, let faith and hope enter first. When your faith leads the way, you will locate the source of your hidden treasures."

— Israelmore Ayivor

TREASURE #1: CALLED TO TEACH

" *My frame was not hidden from You,*
When I was made in secret,
And skillfully wrought in the lowest parts of the earth.
Your eyes saw my substance, being yet unformed.
And in Your book they all were written,
The days fashioned for me,
When as yet there were none of them. "
—Psalms 139:15,16 (NKJV)

Born to Teach

As an only child, I had plenty of alone time. I remember playing "school" in the garage of our white wood-framed house in Fort Worth, Texas. An old, rickety ladder served as my teacher's desk. The worn, flat shelf made for holding the paint can substituted as my bookshelf. I loved reading out loud to my invisible but always attentive students. Neither the sweltering garage during summer nor the cold of winter deterred me from "teaching" them all the wisdom I had gained through fourth grade.

Planting the Seed

Mrs. Grubbs, my fourth-grade teacher, ignited my passion for reading and listening as others read to me. Her jet-black hair, bright-red fingernails, and cheerful laugh lit up our classroom. Every day we begged her to read our favorite book about a mischievous little girl who sits on a bee. As the story developed, her voice became louder and extra animated. At the book's climax, when the little girl sits on the bee, Mrs. Grubbs screamed and plopped in a chair as if she had just sat on the bee. We exploded in laughter! The harder we laughed, the more she laughed, and tears would roll down her pale cheeks. Then all of us laughed even more.

She did more than read aloud; she performed the story by bringing it to life. Reading with expression and animation made the characters come alive. Her teaching style drew us in and helped us trust the plot of the story. When she read the climax, we were living it! Without realizing it, I wanted to be just like Mrs. Grubbs.

An Invitation

My parents and I regularly attended a Methodist church, but they didn't push their beliefs on me. They just made sure I heard God's Word, so I could choose faith for myself.

Our minister baptized me as an infant, and the summer after sixth grade, I prayed to invite Christ to be my Savior. I asked our minister to rebaptize me, which recommitted me and publicly acknowledged my conscious effort to make my faith in Christ the center of my being.

The door to this treasure of faith opened at the closing celebration of a youth group church retreat. There were sixth graders (headed for seventh grade) through high school seniors attending. We enjoyed the zany inside and outside activities all week. The leaders enticed us to attend their Bible camp by making learning fun and exciting.

Even at a young age, I always felt more comfortable with one or two friends than in a large group. It always embarrassed me to be on a stage or in front of a large group of people. But by the end of our week, I felt comfortable on the small stage in our church.

As we sang uplifting hymns, our youth leader began praying out loud. He asked those wanting to confess their sins and ask Christ into their hearts to pray along with him. As I prayed, I felt an odd warmth wash over my insides. Tears stung my eyes and rolled down my face as the current between my heart and mind connected, and I understood why Christ had died for me.

I whispered my sincere requests. "Please forgive me for everything I have done wrong. I believe in You and Your Son and promise to try my hardest to live for You."

Joy and peace were immediate. As I practiced prayer and meditation, asking God what plan He had for my life gained importance. Even as a preteen, I had the sense that teaching or nursing would be my life's work.

Discovering My Niche

Upon entering junior high, I began volunteering with two

different groups of children to get experience in the nursing and teaching fields.

First, I worked as a candy-striper at Fort Worth Children's Hospital. I'm not sure they still call volunteers candy-stripers. Maybe the name came from the white uniform aprons with red stripes like a candy cane.

My jobs included delivering books and toys to children who were too sick or weak to play and read in the communal playroom. For those well enough to come, I entertained and played with them. They loved coming into the bright, colorful area packed full of soft stuffed animals, puzzles, games, and books. I enjoyed working puzzles and playing games with them, but reading to them was my favorite activity. I loved putting expression and life into books, just like Mrs. Grubbs.

When I read Helen Keller's autobiography to the children, it moved me so much I wondered if God wanted me to teach blind children. Being enthralled with the story, I bought the book and finished reading it at home. As I read about Helen's teacher, Anne Sullivan, I asked myself, *How could one teacher single-handedly open a blind, deaf, and dumb child's world and change it forever?*

Then I watched the movie *The Miracle Worker*. Anne Sullivan's creativity, determination, and perseverance opened Helen's window to the world. Anne loved Helen and kept hammering until she broke through Helen's silent and dark prison. She connected with her and taught her how to communicate.

Love, connection, and teaching (in that order) stuck with me.

The next summer, I volunteered with blind children. I was not old enough to drive, so I rode on a bus with the kids to parks, museums, and zoos. They were excited and appreciative, and I enjoyed making a difference.

However, I soon learned the challenges of describing sights, sounds, and smells of animals, objects, and scenery. I said things like, "This gray rhinoceros is about three feet tall and massive." How could I describe the animals to children who had never seen colors or sizes?

My heart was in it, but I began wondering, *Should I teach ALL children, not just blind ones?*

High School

I kept my longing to teach throughout high school, studying religiously to make the best grades possible. From my freshman to senior years, I evaluated which teachers were my favorites.

Why did some of my teachers motivate me more than others? Was it their passion for the subject, teaching style, personality, and connection with their students? Or was it a combination of all these qualities that made them so effective, engaging, and enjoyable? If I became a teacher, which of their qualities could I emulate?

Mrs. Thomas was my favorite high school teacher. Catherine Thomas was quiet, calm, and kind. She taught English, and she fueled my love of language and writing. She shared practical writing strategies that helped me throughout college. I learned a precise and efficient system for outlining before writing and how different types of writing required different tactics.

Her love of language and writing, instruction, and inspiration still speak through everything I teach and write today.

Her kind smile and gentle demeanor became a major part of my teaching style.

Falling in Love

I fell in love with John Granger in Mrs. Thomas's English class. He sat between my friend, Janet, and me. He spent much of his time playing golf for our high school golf team and not as much time studying. He once tried copying from Janet's and my work. I said no (being a follow-the-rules kind of girl). But I sure enjoyed his attention.

One day, I wore a long face as I entered the class, upset about what the dentist had planned for me. I inherited many great qualities from my father, such as his quirky sense of humor and his unique ability to read people. However, inheriting his teeth became my albatross. I had super-thin enamel on my teeth, and my mouth was already full of fillings from cavities.

Our dentist had replaced the white fillings in my front teeth so many times there was not much of the tooth's surface left. When the filling chipped AGAIN, he recommended pulling out my four front teeth and replacing them with a removable bridge!

Today, any dentist would recommend crowns or implants. But my parents were confident this older gentleman knew what he was doing. I hated the prospect of being toothless at seventeen when the bridge wasn't in my mouth.

John asked me what was wrong. When I told him, he looked at me and asked, "Why are you so upset about having front teeth that might look better?"

After I thought about it, I agreed and quit moping. Perhaps John's common-sense approach to life attracted me to him.

I had been dating a football player for about a year and a half. Suddenly, homemade chocolate chip cookies found their way into John's locker on days when I knew he had a golf tournament. With graduation right around the corner, Mrs. Thomas frequently let us leave her class early to eat lunch together. Besides being a talented teacher, she was also a good matchmaker! We began dating just in time to attend our senior dinner dance together.

Marriage and a Career

After graduating from Southwest High School, John earned a scholarship playing golf for North Texas State. He moved into the dormitory in Denton, Texas. I stayed in Fort Worth to attend Texas Wesleyan College. We continued to date on weekends, and we married in our second year of college. I was nineteen years old, and he was twenty.

He had his sites set on playing professional golf after college, so I dug in and graduated in three years by taking summer school and online classes. John's parents let us live rent-free in their modest house, and we both took weekend jobs to make money. He worked as a starter on the first hole at the Colonial Country Club. I worked as an assistant to a professor at TWC. On Saturdays, I worked at Fort Worth Children's Hospital as a receptionist in the Physical Therapy Department.

John's golf scholarship paid for everything, including his dorm room. After we married, the college gave us a monthly stipend to replace his dorm allowance. Luckily for us, both sets of parents lived in Fort Worth. Besides giving us a rent-free place to live, they fed us many free meals and provided a free place to do all our laundry.

Soon after graduating from Texas Wesleyan with a Bachelor of Science degree in Elementary Education, I landed a job teaching kindergarten for a public school in Azle, Texas. It took me forty-five minutes to get to work, but I didn't mind because I loved the kids and staff, and they seemed to like me. The next year, John graduated with a bachelor's degree in business. Since he knew many Colonial Country Club golfers through working there on weekends, he found backers to fund his first year of playing golf in mini-tours.

For one year, he practiced and played in tournaments to make money and get on the pro circuit. I continued teaching kindergarten and loving it. Being on summer vacation from teaching allowed me to travel with John and watch him play.

Life was good.

TREASURE #2: CALLED TO MOTHER

"For I know the thoughts that I think toward you, says the Lord, thoughts of peace and not of evil, to give you a future and a hope."
—Jeremiah 29:11 (NKJV)

Careers and children

At the end of his mini-tour experience, John began working for a savings and loan company in Fort Worth. He hit practice balls after work and enjoyed playing golf with friends on weekends. He played in many prestigious amateur tournaments, many of those in Texas, and some in other states.

While teaching in Azle, Texas, I got pregnant with our first child. I remember always having crackers with me to battle nausea. Walking past the coffee urn each morning was not as appealing as it had been before pregnancy. But once I got into the classroom and started interacting with the kids, I felt better.

Amy was due in November, and John was climbing the ladder in his business. We welcomed the prospect of having a child, so I quit teaching in May to become a full-time mom. I enjoyed being at home, thankful for the time to take naps, and have more energy for all those night-time feedings.

After two years, I felt a gnawing to get back to work. I began substituting in the Fort Worth public elementary schools. It wasn't every day, and I thought it would be the right blend of career and home. I soon learned the pay was much less than teaching full time. Also, it was stressful waiting for the early morning call and going to a new school each time.

This gnawing to teach would not go away. John and I decided we could use the extra money, so I returned to the Azle Schools to teach fifth-grade full time. We were fortunate because Amy stayed with Sissy, one of our sweet sisters-in-law. I enjoyed the fifth graders, but driving from Fort Worth to Azle and back ate up an hour and a half each day. So, the following year, I took a job closer to home teaching fifth grade in Everman, Texas.

During this time in the classroom, I got pregnant with our second child. This pregnancy was harder than the first, as I was super sick for months. As challenging as it was, I loved teaching the fifth graders.

One of my fifth graders that year told me her mom was already caring for an infant in their home while the little girl's parents worked. I visited with her mom, and we decided she would be the perfect babysitter for our baby. Jo was quiet, kind, and loving. Besides, they lived right down the street from the school. Their whole family proved to be a treasure. We became very close and grew to love each one of them.

My students loved being with me and watching my belly grow. They laughed when I rested the teacher manual on my baby shelf. They got more excited as the time drew near for Bart's birth, but it saddened them to know I would not be back for the rest of the school year. I stopped teaching in the middle of March, and our baby was born on March 24, 1981.

It's a Boy

We did not want to find out the sex of our babies before birth, but our doctor knew. At the very last minute, he persuaded John to put on the booties and cap and come into the delivery room. He had taken no classes to prepare, but our close friend, Bart Tompkins, strongly encouraged him to go in. I was in no condition to care, but afterward, he felt grateful he witnessed the birth of his son. We named our son, Bart, after Bart Tompkins.

Bart had a rough entry. He was three weeks early and spent his first twenty-four hours on oxygen in intensive care. Hours after his birth, the doctor suggested we call our minister.

We were so relieved and thankful when he began to breathe on his own. As his lungs developed, he moved from intensive care into the regular baby nursery. It thrilled us when we brought him home from the hospital!

His sister, Amy, was four-and-a-half. She decided she might not want to keep him.

"Mom, can we put him in the trash?" she asked.

But soon, she became a great helper and sister.

Back To Work

I returned to teaching in August. We enrolled Amy in a terrific daycare close to our home. Bart began his two years of staying with Jo. We felt blessed; both children were happy and well cared for, but some things were out of our control.

Bart developed acid reflux and asthma. Reflux occurs when the stomach's acid used to digest our food goes up into the esophagus. A ring of muscle at the opening of the stomach lets food in but typically keeps the acid from coming back up. When this valve fails, severe indigestion occurs. Also, the reflux (which is hereditary, as Amy also had reflux) may set off severe coughing spasms and asthma.

Many nights I met his doctor in the office to get inhalation treatments to control his coughing spasms. We began giving him medication several times a day with a portable nebulizer. This machine followed him to his babysitter's, and she was religious about providing his treatments.

When he was two, we enrolled Bart in the same daycare Amy attended. The nebulizer still followed him. As he got older, he did not need the treatments unless he was sick.

Full-Time Mother

John worked hard to advance in the savings and loan business. He continued practicing his golf and playing in golf tournaments several times a year. Once again, we decided I could stop teaching to stay at home with Amy and Bart.

Amy was starting kindergarten, and life needed to slow down for Bart and me. Although I enjoyed my job, I was burning the candle at both ends as a wife, mother, teacher, homemaker, etc. I looked forward to being at home with Bart, and I wanted to be more available for Amy. I eagerly awaited helping in her classroom and seeing her interact with her new friends.

Priceless Time at Home

My time at home proved to be invaluable. As the plot of my life has unfolded, I am forever grateful I had those years at home to love and care for my family.

We moved to a different neighborhood just as Bart started kindergarten. Amy was in fifth grade, and I could now get involved as a volunteer in their school. I loved sitting with them during lunch and getting to know their friends and teachers.

Both Amy and Bart made friends quickly. Bart was exceptionally fortunate to make friends with neighbors who were his age and went to the same school.

Activities and Interests

Amy's activities included tennis, swimming for the Colonial Country Club swim team, and dance. She was fortunate to have Nancy Brown as her dance instructor. Nancy was a positive role model and a talented teacher, and Amy loved dancing. We enjoyed attending her recitals and performances.

Besides our daughter's activities, my husband and I enjoyed watching our son's T-ball, baseball, and basketball games. Even though he hustled up and down the court, Bart was not a basketball star because he was shorter than most of his friends. But he sure enjoyed playing catcher in little league baseball. Showing promise, our son invested himself in baseball, knowing his dad had also played catcher on baseball teams before starting to play golf. He always wanted to make his father proud of him.

Around the age of ten, golf became Bart's favorite sport. He shared a passion for the game with his dad, who still actively competed in many amateur tournaments each year. Being small kept Bart from hitting the ball long distances off the tee. Because of this, he spent extra hours putting and chipping around the practice green. If his tee shot did not land far enough for him to par a hole, his short game helped make up the difference. As his putting and chipping continued to improve, he focused more of his energy and passion on golf.

We spent precious hours and made lasting memories traveling to summer golf tournaments with Bart and his friends. Various moms and dads would take turns chaperoning the boys, dictated by who could take off from work or who was available.

I'll never forget an American Junior Golf Association (AJGA) tournament in Aspen, Colorado, for which I quickly volunteered. Only the top-notch junior players received an invitation to play in the AJGA tournaments. Bart was proud and excited to participate. We flew to Aspen, and it pelted rain every day. But the boys played on, trudging through the soggy fairways and overgrown roughs, posting higher scores than they wanted. Even though Bart felt disappointed with his performance, we had fun spending time together and making precious memories.

Golf Team Bound

As a freshman in high school, Bart's desire to be on the varsity golf team became a reality. His talent, his dad's invaluable coaching, and his many hours of practice earned him a spot on the five-man varsity team. In September 1996, he played in his first Dr. Pepper/Paschal Invitational high school golf tournament, which his high school sponsored.

The history of this golf tournament went back forty-plus years. Initially, the city sponsored it and called it the Parks and Recreation tournament. There were two divisions, a high school and a college division, and years before, Bart's dad had played in both.

Then in the early 1990s, Paschal High School and their golf coach, Herb Stephens, took on the responsibility of hosting the tournament for many of the high school boys' teams in Texas.

In 1996, the name changed to Dr. Pepper/Paschal Invitational, but only for two years.

A Stumbling Block

Shortly after playing in this fall tournament, Bart complained of severe wrist pain to the point of not being able to swing a golf club. After multiple x-rays and doctor visits with our family doctor and a specialist, we learned he had a wrist disease called Kienbock's disease.

This disease is a rare condition (affecting fewer than 200,000 people in the U.S.) in which a small wrist bone loses its blood supply and eventually dies. This causes pain and stiffness when moving the wrist. If the disease worsens, the bone can collapse, and the other bones in the wrist may move. Research shows trauma to the wrist might cause this disease. [1]

After hearing this depressing news, we remembered Bart had complained of wrist pain while playing catcher in little league baseball. At the time, it never seemed severe enough (or so we thought) to take him to the doctor.

His hand specialist told us he might never play golf again! This news crushed us because we knew how much Bart wanted to play high school golf. His dad vehemently explained to the surgeon the reasons Bart HAD to play golf. He was not cut out for an executive's job behind a desk, but rather a talented and committed golfer. We begged the surgeon for options so he could play again.

After researching and conferring with other doctors, the specialist met with all three of us to share the possibility of surgery, which MIGHT increase blood flow to the lunate bone, the one being crushed and starved for blood.

If he shortened the ulna bone in Bart's arm and immobilized it in a cast, the pressure might be less on the wrist. This procedure could allow the compressed lunate bone to get more oxygen resulting in healing. Two surgeries would be necessary–one to shorten the bone and insert screws, and another to remove them. Bart would be in a cast for months and miss golf for the rest of the school year!

We were thankful and hopeful this could work. All three of us, especially Bart, agreed to both surgeries. Giving up golf for the rest of his freshman year sounded better than giving it up forever!

Herb Stephens

Bart had tremendous respect for his golf coach, Herb Stephens. Coach did his part in making sure Bart stayed physically fit and mentally strong for that moment the doctors cleared him to play golf again.

Coach Stephens was a successful teacher and coach because of his discipline, high expectations, and love for his students and players. Through the years, he led many of his golfers from okay to better to great. He required a lot of physical training: lifting weights, sit-ups, pushups, running, etc.

Bart loved Coach's sense of humor, and his sometimes gruff exterior never scared him off. Instead, Bart followed Coach around as if he were his assistant. Since Bart could not run, Coach required him to do sit-ups, hundreds of them! Of course, Bart never told us he was doing them or complained.

When Bart had to write an essay for a freshman English class assignment, he wrote the following. The title is *His Great Intentions*. (This paper is his handwriting, and you can see his teacher's comments.)

Bart Granger   Mrs. Dudek
English III - 3   9-4-96

His Great Intentions

As I walked into that classroom on an especially hot August afternoon I saw him for the first time. As I listened it was very clear to me what he expected. This was nothing less than each and everyones personal best. He said he would prepare us mentally and physically ready for our ultimate goal as a team, the state title.

He explained to the team that it would take more work and effort than ever before. I had no idea of how deep this last statement really went. He went along to say that we would be on a regular physical training program which would include weights, running, and situps. He also said to obtain the title we could not have any distractions. If the case, the person who caused the distraction would have to run to the tandy center which was a ten-mile run. He also said our team had to come together to get there. Well we really kind of fell short in that category I was out for the majority of fall with a

severe wrist injury. But I was fortunate
enough to be able to compete in the spring.
When the regional tournament came around
we lost another player due to grades and
were forced to play four strong and know
that our score was going to count. We
went in to the tournament trying to
do our best and see where it takes us. tense
After the first day we found ourselves
holding a three stroke lead. In my opinion
we got a little over confident and decreased
our chances by a change in attitudes. Before
we played in the final round Coach Stephens
warned us we still need to play a very good
round in order to win. Well when the scores
were tallied we found ourselves six shots out
of our dream, out of the state tournament.
Suddenly we went from high to low in a matter
of less than 24 hours. Standing up to recieve
that third place award might have been the
worst feeling ever to wash across my body.
That is when I noticed how the team
really worked. We all felt the pain of losing
and the underclassman felt the pain as well
as the hunger to try at it again. On that

four hour bus ride home I experienced and
relived to my self what I had learned.
     Coach Stephens taught us about life
and how we should live it. Through him we
felt winning, losing, pain, joy, happiness, madness,
and most of all the hunger to be the best
Through the next 3 years I am sure I
will learn more and more from this man I
call Coach. Good.

What Now?

Except for chipping and putting with one arm, Bart's golf-related activities had stopped. Looking for other things to fill his time, he became more active in Young Life. This program met at our church one night a week to share the opportunity with all high school kids to meet Jesus and follow Him.[2] College students who volunteer to be leaders and adult mentors help staff Young Life. Both the adults and the volunteers visit the students where they spend most of their time—in school, at sporting events, and in the shopping malls. They strive to build relationships of trust with kids from all backgrounds. The weekly lessons at their gatherings include music, outlandish skits, and biblical applications/stories. Their purpose is to engage high school students and to make them think about their lives and their faith. The sessions are zany, entertaining, and thought-provoking.

Young Life also sponsors summer camps and winter ski trips. In the fall of 1996, Bart started "working" on me for permission to go snow skiing during Christmas break. FUNNY KID! He wanted to go with his arm in a cast on a two-day bus ride there, four days of skiing, and another two-day ride back home?

As God would have it, I was hosting Bible studies and small group prayer sessions in our home with female college students from TCU. Most of them volunteered with Young Life.

One of the female leaders called and asked if I would volunteer as a counselor on the ski trip. Her grandmother was very ill, and she did not want to leave her to go on the trip.

Having taught fifth and sixth graders, and thinking ninth-grade girls couldn't be a lot different, I began considering it. At least a parent would be there for Bart in case he got hurt. Little did I know this one event would propel me on a path I would need.

I climbed on the girls' bus with my bag and pillow at five a.m., noticing the girls staring at me. From the looks on their faces, I imagined they were wondering, "Who is this old lady getting on our bus?"

As I settled into a seat at the front of the bus, the girls began to realize they had a new chaperone. By the cautious looks on their faces, I assumed they were hoping they would be in the younger counselor's group! Seeing their "warm" greeting, I began to panic and wondered if I had made a mistake.

Once on the road, their adorable college-aged leader introduced me to the girls and told them why I was there. Their empathy for their "real" counselor's reason for missing the trip helped break the ice.

We all settled in for the seventeen-hour bus ride to Breckenridge, Colorado. My primary duties included:

- staying especially close to one girl who had diabetes to make sure she had instant access to her medications
- making sure no boys entered the girls' room
- facilitating nightly discussions with my girls after the skits and lessons.

These rich, nightly discussions allowed me to share Bible verses and true personal experiences. This precious sharing time opened us all to prayer, learning about each other, and learning about Christ's gifts.

I am NOT a minister. My knowledge of Scripture comes only from my church participation, time spent in Bible Study Fellowship (BSF)—which is a treasure all its own—and my time spent reading the Bible.

When one of our discussions became SERIOUS, sensing that one girl wanted to know how to become a true believer in Christ, I panicked!

Was I equipped to answer her questions? Wasn't there someone else I might ask to help her? Suddenly, a Bible verse popped into my brain.

> *"That if you confess with your mouth the Lord Jesus and believe in your heart that God has raised Him from the dead, you will be saved."*—Romans 10:9 (NKJV)

She read it in her Bible, she believed, she confessed her sins and need for Jesus, and we prayed. Her experience awed me and inspired the Young Life staff and leadership (they also had similar stories to tell). We all encouraged her to tell her parents and her minister when she returned home.

We all made it back safely, including my son. The boys' bus broke down and caused a delay, so we arrived exhausted about two hours late. What a difference a week had made! I had tons of fun skiing and being with the kids, and the girls enjoyed our time together.

My girls attended a different high school from Bart, and they started calling him to rave about the fun they had on the ski trip. Bart shared the girls' positive comments with me. He pretended to act surprised, but I could tell he was pleased and proud. I tried to enlighten him that they were just calling because they missed talking to HIM!

Back to the Classroom

In January, a friend called and asked me to teach part-time at Southwest Christian School. The school needed a sixth-grade teacher for social studies, math, and Bible classes. My geography and map skills are not the best, my math expertise is lacking, and I did not feel equipped to teach the Bible.

My husband reminded me that attending Bible Study Fellowship and studying the Bible had undoubtedly helped prepare me. After thinking and praying about it, I realized my elementary education training and teaching experience could get me through the rest. After all, it was just part-time for half a day.

My son was my second biggest encourager. Our daughter, Amy, was away in Austin, Texas, enjoying her freshman year at the University of Texas. She was focusing her energy on pledging a sorority and working to keep a positive balance between studying and the social expectations of sorority life.

Bart supported his dad's rationale. He asked, "Mom, why wouldn't you want to get back into teaching? Amy is at UT, I am at school all day, and those GIRLS will not stop telling me how awesome you are!"

This part-time teaching job worked into a full-time position the next year. I continued to teach sixth-grade math, social studies, and Bible to two groups each day in this non-denominational private school. This treasure would soon become my ANCHOR.

TREASURE #3: CALLED TO GROW

"So then faith comes by hearing, and hearing by the word of God."
— Romans 10:17 (NKJV)

Examples of Faith

Many faithful friends and loved ones have led the way and opened doors for my faith journey.

Remembering all the weekends I spent the night with my paternal grandmother, Maw, brings sunny smiles to my face. I still enjoy treasured memories of helping her bake Rice Crispy Treats and watching her eat a grapefruit each morning with a pointed spoon. This spoon was perfect for digging out the meat and not having to eat the bitter white part. She would be proud to know I have carried on her tradition. I now eat a grapefruit half almost every morning with a pointed spoon I found at a thrift store.

Maw was a widow and lived in Fort Worth with her two spinster sisters, Auntie and Ettie. They were always eager to sit and talk with me about anything I chose. They taught me how to play Solitaire and Gin Rummy. When we were not playing Gin Rummy together, we all had our Solitaire games going on simultaneously.

My grandmother loved to read and sew, and she liked to give me books to read. When she gave me *To Kill a Mockingbird*, my mother took it away because since I was only ten years old, she thought I was not old enough to read it.

Every Sunday, Maw attended a Baptist church in downtown Fort Worth. I would dress up and go with her. We always sat in the same spot on the right side of the sanctuary with the same people sitting around us. I listened and sang along with the traditional hymns, trying to focus on the sermon.

Looking back, I think I concentrated more on the meat of the sermons with her than when I attended my church and sat next to my parents. I wanted her to be proud of me, so I listened.

I often watched her read and study her Bible at home. I do not remember seeing her pray, but as strong as her faith was, I am sure she prayed in the privacy of her bedroom.

I remember all the times she told me, "When I die, do not be sad! I am going to heaven, where I will be so much happier and healthier than I am now. As you stand at my coffin and look down at me, remember how much better off I am!"

Maybe it was her strong belief in heaven, attending church with her, watching her read her own Bible, or a combination of all three that nourished my faith.

She died when I was in my early twenties. Amy was around two years old. I am pleased Maw met her, and a little sad she never got to see Bart. I still miss her, but her faith and love live in my heart forever.

I have more than one of the Bibles she used. The one containing all the family's birth and death records is especially dear to me. It occupies a special place in my home on top of an antique sewing machine. Even though this old sewing machine is not hers, a time-worn baptismal dress in a shadow box frame hangs on the wall above it. A faded note on an index card explains the dress was made on the first sewing machine to come to Fort Worth, Texas. We found the dress folded in a cardboard box after her death.

An Incredible Story

Before my dad died, he and I spent hours talking as he shared personal stories with me of his upbringing and his time in the Navy during WWII. He was the youngest of four (two older brothers and one older sister), so he had a special bond with his mother.

During one of those special times with him, he told me a story his mother had shared with him. When he was born, Maw had life-threatening complications during childbirth. She flatlined. The doctors thought she was dead, but she came back.

Maw shared her memories of what happened while she was "gone." She told my dad she remembered being in heaven, especially the peaceful beauty and how happy she felt. She was told she could not stay there, and she shared how she did NOT want to come back. Her request was obviously denied, as she returned to live many more years. I did not hear this story until I was in my late forties.

No wonder my grandmother had such a strong belief in heaven! I am so thankful she shared her faith with me as a young child. The way she lived her life according to her beliefs is a stronghold that helps my faith continue to grow.

A Special Invitation

During my "stay at home" time, a persistent and patient friend asked me to join a non-denominational ladies' Bible study group called Bible Study Fellowship. Lynne was our neighbor and friend. We spent many hours visiting while her two sons and Bart played together. Her oldest son, Brent, was Bart's age, and Wade was a little younger. Brent and Bart were in the same class in school. She invited me to the bible study guest day in the fall and spring every year for five years in a row!

My excuses were always plausible: playing in a golf tournament, going to lunch with a friend, volunteering at the kids' school, going to a doctor or dentist appointment, etc. She hung in there, and my life's course changed for the better.

Bible Study Fellowship

I attended BSF for six years, meeting with hundreds of women each Wednesday during the school year. We listened to a lecture, met with a small group of fifteen women to discuss the lesson, and took ten pages of reading and study questions home to answer before the next week.

The Bible was the only resource we could use to complete our homework. I read, prayed, and wrote the answers so I could take part in the small group discussion the following week. If you did not complete your homework, you could not TALK during the small group time!

Also, attendance was mandatory. If you missed too many weekly sessions in a row, you were out... waiting for the next season's guest day to start the process again. I am thankful BSF had these rules in place to hold me accountable. My faith grew stronger because I was more serious about attending and learning.

During those six years, I learned more about the Bible and prayer than I had experienced before. Growing up in the Methodist church, I was familiar with many stories in The New Testament. But I did not understand the importance of the history of God's love and faithfulness to His people in the Old Testament. So, I particularly enjoyed reading those books in the Bible.

As I learned more, I prayed more. As I prayed more, my thoughts, words, and actions began to change. Studying and praying became more and more important to me, and I continued to attend for six years.

Looking back, my commitment had three concrete payoffs:

1. My faith grew by reading the Bible and praying daily. I had to think (and question) as I was reading.
2. My son prayed to accept Christ into his heart when he was ten years old.
3. My studies helped prepare me to teach Bible at Southwest Christian School.

Bart's Spiritual Awakening

In the Methodist church, parents baptize their infants as a promise to raise them in a Christian home. So, we baptized both our daughter and son as infants in our church.

Ten years later, on June 23, 1991, Bart came into my bedroom to find me stretched out on the bed reading my Bible and answering the next week's Bible study questions. He began asking me in-depth questions about how to KNOW he would go to heaven. I shared three verses with him I would not have remembered if I had not been in Bible Study Fellowship.

> *"But we are all like an unclean thing, And all our righteousnesses are like filthy rags; We all fade as a leaf, And our iniquities, like the wind, have taken us away."*
> — Isaiah 64:6 (NKJV)

> *"For God so loved the world that He gave His only begotten Son, that whoever believes in Him should not perish but have everlasting life."*
> —John 3:16 (NKJV)

And the same verse I would later share with a ninth- grader who asked the same questions:

> *"that if you confess with your mouth the Lord Jesus and believe in your heart that God has raised Him from the dead, you will be saved."*
> — Romans 10:9 (NKJV)

I remember discussing with Bart how God is perfect and sinless and we are NOT. Any sin separates us from being in His presence. Only through believing we need the perfect sacrifices Christ made on our behalf is it possible for us to be with God:

- through His Holy Spirit while living on Earth
- through Christ's sacrifices while living in Eternity.

Then I waited... for Bart to say something. I can still see his bright, understanding eyes and the resolve on his face when he said, "Mom, I want to accept Christ's sacrifices, so I can know I will go to heaven."

Enough said... we prayed together for God to please forgive Bart's sins and to fill him with His Spirit because of what Christ had already done. Bart invited Jesus into his heart and life.

Thank you, God, for this pure treasure. Out of all the examples of your faithfulness I am writing about in this book, I thank You for letting me share this moment with my son. I know I will see him again and spend eternity in his presence.

PART TWO: THE MAZE

*"Through the Lord's mercies we are not consumed,
Because His compassions fail not.
They are new every morning;
Great is Your faithfulness."*
— Lamentations 3:22,23 (NKJV)

TREASURE #4: CALLED TO GRIEVE

" Let not your heart be troubled. you believe in God,
believe also in Me.
In My Father's house are many mansions; if it were
not so, I would have told you. I go to prepare a
place for you. "
— John 14:1,2 (NKJV)

Thursday, October 9, 1997

How can so much rain be possible? It had rained for almost two weeks straight, and as I drove home from a full day of teaching, it thrilled me to see sunshine peeking through the clouds! It was also my birthday, and I looked forward to going out to dinner with my whole family.

Our daughter was coming home from Austin for the Texas-OU football game weekend. Sadly, one of her high school friends had died, and she was coming home one day early to attend his funeral on Friday.

As I neared our home, the most vibrant rainbow I had ever

seen shone right over our neighborhood! It seemed to grow out of the ground on the left and make its broad, colorful arc right over our house. It faded out just before it touched the ground on the right side.

I stopped the car on the edge of the street, bowed my head, and prayed, thanking God for the blessings of the rainbow, my family, and my birthday.

Dinner at my favorite Italian restaurant was delicious and entertaining. We enjoyed relaxing with both children, as we all shared our recent experiences, challenges, hopes, and plans with each other.

I remember Bart especially appreciated talking to his sister and listening to her advice on some "friendship issues." Since Bart was sixteen and Amy was nearly twenty-one, the four-and-a-half-year difference was becoming less of a barrier. That evening proved to be a precious bonding moment for our entire family.

Back at home and knowing Friday would be busy, we all prepared for bed. Before going to bed, I knocked on Bart's bedroom door to thank him for spending time with us on my birthday.

What I saw, and the words he said to me, permanently etched themselves in my memory: Standing up, phone in hand, his hair tousled, in his jockeys, talking with his girlfriend, he said, "NO PROBLEM, MOM."

Friday, October 10, 1997

Those were the last words I heard Bart speak. He and I were up early the next morning. He was leaving early to take a makeup test he had missed while playing in a golf tournament. I was midway in my preparation for school when I heard the front door shut.

Being sixteen, he had inherited his sister's car and enjoyed the freedom of driving himself to school.

STILL RAINING! It took me a bit of extra time to get to work because of the dismal weather. Some of my sixth-grade students were late, but we started the day with our usual attendance check, Pledge of Allegiance, and prayer. Then we dove into the curriculum with a twenty-minute Bible lesson on *faith* vs. *fear*.

The principal's assistant interrupted our lesson by standing in the doorway, motioning for me to come to the door. Her look of fear and dismay were painfully evident as she said, "You need to come to the office. There is a nurse from the hospital on the phone. Apparently, your son has been in an accident."

In a daze, I remember walking to the front of the classroom to explain what I knew of the situation. I then drew a road splitting into two paths, labeling them faith and fear, and circling the faith "road."

I found out later that Ben, one of my sixth-grade students, had walked quietly to the front of the room to lead a prayer for Bart and me.

The students had met Bart when he picked me up in the school parking lot after a two-night and three-day class trip to Mo Ranch in Hunt, Texas, only a few weeks before.

This excursion had been my first official teacher trip as a chaperone... six hours on a bus with forty sixth-graders and Kathy, my fellow teacher. Each year the students looked forward to the three days and two nights of outdoor learning activities, science lessons with real reptiles, owl pellet dissection sessions, and group sporting activities such as canoeing, swimming, and volleyball. Parent volunteers bunked with the boys, and we slept (Ha!) with the girls. Then another six hours back home on the bus, and I was one whipped puppy.

I still remember the Friday night Bart picked me up in the school parking lot. I introduced him to my students and their parents until he became impatient to quit meeting people and get out of there.

Settling back into a routine, I began washing dishes (my husband was out of town, and a few plates had piled up in the kitchen sink). Bart came up behind me and began expounding on what had happened in his life while I was at Mo Ranch.

Being exhausted, it tempted me to say, "Bart, can we talk tomorrow?" But deep inside my soul, knowing I should listen, I made a sincere attempt!

Thank you, God, for clueing me in my son needed me, and I would need to hear every word he was willing to share.

The Dreaded Phone Call

When I got to the office, I spoke to a calm, level-voiced nurse. She shared with me my son had been in an accident. She asked, "Is your son dark-headed and about 5'5" tall? Is his name Bart Granger?"

My heart dropped to my stomach. In a fog, I answered, "Yes."

"You need to come to the hospital. Is there someone who can drive you?" the nurse asked. "Whatever you do, take your time and drive carefully."

In my heart, I knew her words were as foreboding as the gray skies had been on my way to work that morning.

My principal, Pam Womack, was standing close to me and immediately offered to drive me wherever I needed to go. I called my husband, and he said he would meet me at the hospital. Our close friend, Vicki, went to our house and brought Amy there.

On the way to the hospital, Pam drove me up to the front of Bart's school. I got out and ran into the office to ask if Bart was there. Sweet Hillary, a friend of Bart's who was volunteering in the office, sadly answered, "No, he is not in class."

His golf coach, Herb Stephens, rounded the corner and said, "I'm going to the hospital. I will meet you there. Do you have someone to drive you?"

"Yes," I answered. "My principal is driving me."

Sights and Sounds of a Tragedy

Sights and sounds of a disaster met us as we converged on the hospital's trauma emergency reception area. My husband and daughter arrived just as we did. An ambulance, police officer, and a young man's face I recognized, but could not place, were the first things and people I saw. The young man was older than Bart. He was Amy's age, and his mom was there. I recognized her from my Bible Study Fellowship days; she had been a discussion group leader. Why were they here?

Two doctors whisked John, Amy, and I into a private sitting area where the answers would soon unfold.

1. The young man I saw was the cousin of the boy driving the truck Bart was riding in.
2. There were three boys in the accident: the driver

who was being treated in another area of the hospital, another friend of Bart's, who was taken to a nearby children's hospital, and Bart, who was being treated in this hospital's trauma emergency unit.

3. We could not see Bart because of the seriousness of his injuries.
4. They had done a tracheostomy to provide his organs with oxygen, but his brain swelled and was unresponsive.
5. If the swelling went down, then there was a SLIGHT possibility he might improve.
6. He was unconscious and was not in any pain.

I remember asking the somber young doctor, "Can Bart die?"

He answered, "Yes, if his brain cannot recover. Please know we are doing everything we can to save him. We have him connected to every possible machine to help him. I am so very sorry."

Years later, Bart's dad and I would meet the trauma nurse who was at Bart's side on the day of the accident. She shared with us how the young intern who answered our questions in the waiting room came back to the trauma room and cried.

TREASURE #5: CALLED TO TRUST

"Even though I walk
through the darkest valley,
I will fear no evil,
for you are with me;
your rod and your staff,
they comfort me."
— Psalm 23:4 (NKJV)

My Morning Devotional

After six years in Bible Study Fellowship, I learned how differently I reacted to life's daily stresses when I started the day reading my Bible. I had committed to taking some time before school to "feed" myself, to be better equipped to listen to the students and answer their questions.

On October 10, I was using a devotional guide called Our Daily Bread.[1] The verses told of a follower of Christ named Stephen. He was boldly declaring Christ as the Son of God to those who betrayed and murdered Him.

"When they heard these things they were cut to the heart, and they gnashed at him with their teeth. But he, being full of the Holy Spirit, gazed into heaven and saw the glory of God, and Jesus standing at the right hand of God, and said, "Look! I see the heavens opened and the Son of Man standing at the right hand of God!" Then they cried out with a loud voice, stopped their ears, and ran at him with one accord. and they cast him out of the city and stoned him. And the witnesses laid down their clothes at the feet of a young man named Saul. And they stoned Stephen as he was calling on God and saying, "Lord Jesus, receive my spirit." Then he knelt down and cried out with a loud voice, "Lord, do not charge them with this sin."And when he had said this, he fell asleep."
— Acts 7:54-59 (NKJV)

I remember questioning,"Why did God allow Stephen to SEE heaven? How did Stephen forgive the men stoning him when it was such a painful and brutal death?"

Answers to Questions

The answers to my questions came when I saw the parents of the young man who had been driving the truck Bart was riding in. I also began to realize why the police officer was still there.

My mind and heart reeled in turmoil as a second doctor

came to the waiting room to explain Bart's injuries in greater detail. He told us Bart's brain swelled at impact so quickly it blocked the blood flow and oxygen to his organs. Since he had arrived at the hospital, there had been no brain activity. They had immediately performed a tracheostomy (a hole in the windpipe) to ensure the rest of his organs were still receiving oxygen to keep them alive.

My questions were, "Is he in any pain? Will the brain recover?"

He assured all three of us Bart felt no pain. Because of the swelling, he probably did not feel pain when he "flew" out of his friend's truck and hit his head.

The doctor promised to give us updates and to let us know if Bart showed signs of any brain activity. By law, the hospital had to keep him on life support for several more hours to give his brain a chance to recover.

After meeting with the doctor, we left the dark, private room to face multitudes of precious friends and relatives who were gathering in the halls of the hospital. Out of concern and love for our family, Bart's high school friends and Amy's friends and their parents were filling the hallways.

Fortunately, when the hospital instructed us to vacate the hallways due to privacy laws, Amy's closest friend's mom asked the hospital if we could move to a large "meeting room" where people could congregate to comfort each other and wait for updates.

They agreed, everyone hustled into a large room, and soon her husband went to a local barbecue restaurant and brought back trays of barbecue for friends and relatives to eat.

Being Ministered To

In another smaller meeting room, our minister took both of my hands in his and began to speak comforting words, which the Spirit was dictating. I shared the devotional I had read that morning, and the verse I was hanging onto for dear life:

> *"In My Father's house are many mansions; if it were*
> *not so, I would have told you. I go to prepare a*
> *place for you."*
> — John 14:2 (NKJV)

I remember one very close friend taking my hands and with tears in his eyes, asking, "What are we going to do?"

"We will accept what happens and trust God either way," I answered. He stared blankly at me like I was off my rocker....

I saw so many faces, some of which I did not recognize at first. It was so odd to see so many people from all walks of our lives assembled in this one place.

Bart's dad, sister, and I went into the chapel and prayed. I don't remember if my prayers were silent or vocalized, but I do remember what I prayed. None of us wanted Bart to live with severe brain damage, so I prayed God would let us know if it was time for Him to take Bart home. None of us could bear the thought of deciding to turn off Bart's life support.

My memories of the timing are still blurry, but around one in the afternoon, it was becoming more apparent Bart was not improving. Struggling with the burden of who would decide whether to unplug his life support, I asked the doctor. He kindly explained our son was NOT in a coma... his brain was dead to all activities his body and organs would need to improve. If he did not show changes by mid-afternoon, there would be no decision to make. This searing pain our family and friends all felt was a blessing and a burden. I felt a responsibility to keep them updated and to reassure them.

Ministering to Others

As I entered the large meeting room to explain the news, there were few seats for them and only one table the food occupied. They were standing or sitting on the floor in clusters and talking quietly or whispering. Some were leaning against the walls for physical and emotional support. A hush fell over the room as I entered with John and Amy close behind.

Sharing the doctor's dismal news with them, I vaguely remember what I told them next: "If God is big enough to take Bart early, He is big enough to get us through this."

I remember saying a prayer, and we left that room for the last time.

Seeing Bart

The next communication we had with the doctor was later in the afternoon. They moved Bart out of the trauma unit into a private room. The doctors invited us to go into his room to see him and to spend time with him. Once again, they told us there was still no brain activity.

The upcoming scenes are etched in my soul and are the most painful for me to put on paper. A soft-spoken representative from Life Gift met us in the hallway and gently asked us if we would consider donating Bart's organs. The response time was short... "Definitely" was our answer.

They explained they would remove all organs not damaged by the accident and cautiously asked if we would be willing also to donate tissue and skin. Burn victims and those needing neck and spinal surgeries would benefit. We gave permission for them to use anything that could help someone else. They explained there would be no additional cost to us, and they assured us the process would be as reverent as possible.

A few days later, when we looked inside Bart's billfold, we saw he had signed up for organ donation on his driver's license. Seeing this confirmed we had made the right decision.

Hand in hand, Amy, John, and I walked in to find Bart lying on a bed, eyes closed, and looking surprisingly serene and very much like himself. There were very few tubes attached—only IVs and the tracheostomy tube to provide the oxygen necessary to keep his vital organs alive. His face had no bruises or scratches, and his handsome features were still intact.

I remember wondering, "Is his spirit already gone? He looks so peaceful! Does he know we are all standing around him? Can he hear what we are saying?"

My sudden jolt back to reality came when my mother entered the room. My father and several other loved ones waited in the hall, choosing not to come in; they wanted to remember Bart as he looked the last time they saw him. My mother began to wail, ordering Bart not to die. At that point, my body's physical shock took over, and I raced to the private bathroom inside his room.

Someone gave me a cold compress to put on my head as

my intestines unloaded only a portion of the pain, panic, and torment I had been enduring all day.

I heard people usher my mother out of the room, and I could eventually return to Bart's bedside.

Crying and trembling as I attempt to put these memories into words, I remember praying out loud and rubbing my hand over Bart's thick eyebrows (we teased him about his unibrow. I always envied those dense, dark eyebrows since I have always been sparse in the eyebrow department). I leaned over and kissed his face, reminded him how much I loved him and walked out of the room.

Blessings Abound

Blessings abound! As we left his room, knowing they would soon remove Bart's life support, we saw the dad of one of Bart's friends in a white hospital coat waiting for us in the hallway. He is a well-respected heart surgeon and would be the one to remove Bart's heart for organ donation. God used him to comfort us with the news Bart did not suffer. I am thankful it took only one-and-a-half to two minutes for his brain to swell from the impact of the wreck, so he did not have time to feel pain or sorrow.

He also shared he had examined Bart, and his heart was beating strongly. The accident had not damaged it. I knew this kind, Christian doctor would be loving and gentle. After all, he had a son who was Bart's age and knew him.

TREASURE #6: CALLED TO LIVE

"Because I live, you will live also."
—John 14:19 (NKJV)

The Trek Home

Hand in hand, my husband, daughter, and I walked out of the hospital, down the sidewalk, and around the building to find the place where John had parked our car earlier that day.

How is it possible for SO MUCH TO CHANGE in only a few hours?

None of us spoke on the journey home... there was nothing to say.

By that evening, relatives, friends, and neighbors packed our house. Many dropped by with food or just to hug and love on us. Perhaps some came just to verify Bart was not there.

The bulk of the visitors were friends of Amy and Bart. Many of them, especially Amy's college friends, spent the night or came back early the next day.

Oddly enough, I remember having an enormous desire to welcome, comfort, and feed every person who came to console us. God gave me the energy to be hospitable, kind, and upbeat; He was calling me to LIVE. When exhaustion set in, I would retreat to my bedroom, lie down on the bed, and stare into space, soaking up the quiet solace. I remember inviting my college roommate, whom I had not seen in years, to come to my room to visit and get caught up. Then after a few minutes, we reentered the living and dining rooms, only to find more friends and relatives.

The Next Few Days

In the next few days, we "hung" between arranging the details for the end of a life and doing what was necessary to keep living ours.

I ate very little, but I had no problem sleeping. A common question from concerned friends was, "Are you getting enough sleep?"

My answer was, "Yes, I could sleep all day."

At least when I slept, the pain disappeared.

Out-of-Town Friends

Two very close friends, Bart and Janet, who lived in Colorado, rang our doorbell the day after Bart died. My first thought when I opened the door and saw them standing there was, "What are you doing here?" Then, after a few moments of awkward silence, I remembered, and we embraced as tears streamed down our faces.

For years, our family had taken an annual summer pilgrimage to their home in Ft. Collins, Colorado, where John and big Bart (as we affectionately called him) played in their member-guest golf tournament. Our son was a baby, and Amy was around four or five when we started driving from Fort Worth to Colorado.

John and I graduated from high school with both Bart and Janet, but we did not become close friends until Bart phoned John and asked him if we would come to Colorado for his Member-Guest golf tournament.

They had two sons who were older than our children, but our families had tons of fun together. The cooler climate, the panoramic mountains, time with the kids at the swimming pool, and the men winning the tournament were reasons we returned each summer.

Who wouldn't want a week of cooler weather and the company of great friends? We became so close we named our son after Bart; we chose John Barton Granger for his name, and we called him Bart.

To keep the two names separate when we visited them, we called them "Big Bart" and "Little Bart." Big Bart is the friend who persuaded John to go into the delivery room when Little Bart was born!

A few years before our son died, Big Bart had lived through the horrors of colon cancer and a colostomy. About a year after Little Bart's death, we learned his cancer had returned elsewhere and had traveled to his brain.

Big Bart's will to live and sense of humor were endless as he was in and out of the hospital, experiencing the ravaging effects of cancer treatments. After torturous pain and suffering for him and his family, God gave him relief and called him home.

I am still encouraged thinking about how great the day must have been when the two Barts met again for eternity!

Planning a Funeral

Funeral arrangements are always traumatic, but ours were less so because Trey, our funeral director (who was also a relative on my husband's side), did his best to bring the arrangements to us. He sat with us in our TV room with our minister and one of Bart's friends and golf teammates, Adam, to plan the celebration of Bart's life.

We decided whether to bury or cremate him after our daughter boldly stated,

"We can't bury him in the ground with a bunch of old people!"

After laughing a little and thinking, *Well said*, we chose a closed casket service with cremation to follow.

The funeral director asked us what kind of container we wanted to put Bart's ashes in, and we told him we did not want anything fancy. We knew we would not keep them in the container. Instead, we would distribute them outside in the open.

We scheduled his service for October 13. This date was significant because Bart's favorite hole at the golf course where he and his dad played was the thirteenth.

It was the first par three he could hit in regulation (land his first shot on the green), and this was challenging because his tee shot had to go over water. Bart and his dad often placed bets for Slurpees on that hole and always challenged each other to see who would be first to get a hole-in-one. Bart scared the hole a few times but never made a hole-in-one. John never got one either, but he always paid for the Slurpees.

It concerned our minister that our sanctuary would not hold enough people. Another denomination's minister contacted him to offer his church's sanctuary. After discussing this as a family, we decided Bart would want to be in his home church, and we would feel more comfortable there.

The Day Arrives

What do I remember from the day of Bart's funeral?

- I remember our ride in the limo and discussing the significance of having the funeral on the thirteenth, because of the connection between Bart and his dad.
- We entered the main door of the church (there was no side entrance) and trudged down to the front of the sanctuary with everyone staring at us.
- I saw people in folding chairs packed into a room next to the main auditorium, and when I saw them, I smiled and gave them a thumbs-up sign.
- I remember the comforting, uplifting music. We had chosen some contemporary Christian songs and some traditional hymns, especially my favorite hymn, "Great is Thy Faithfulness."

Two close friends gave touching eulogies that were heart-felt and beautiful. Herb Stephens, Bart's golf coach, announced in his eulogy the high school golf tournament in Fort Worth, Texas, would now be called the Bart Granger Memorial Golf Tournament. Lastly, our minister spoke his thoughts and God's comfort.

After the service was over, a multitude of people lined up to talk to us. I remember little about what I said....

After most of the attendees had left, we walked outside. Bart's simple casket waited in the back of a hearse, and I took two white roses on Bart's casket (I still have the dried rose petals in a heart-shaped crystal dish), kissed the temporary box that held him, and we got back in the limo to go home.

We later learned when they could not seat any more people in the sanctuary or the outlying rooms around it, the overflow of friends stood outside the front door and just listened.

A Week Later

Trey, the funeral director, delivered Bart's ashes about a week later. Even though we had not wanted them to be in a "fancy" container, we had to LAUGH when we saw what held them.

He admitted he was a little embarrassed to deliver them this way. They were in a round cardboard container inside a large, plastic zip-lock bag. The container reminded me of the cardboard tubs the ice cream stores used to hold the flavors they scooped!

I can't reveal where we put his ashes (since it was probably illegal), but a few of them remained in Bart's golf bag. They would soon travel with his golf team to the regional and state high school golf tournaments the following spring.

In the days and weeks following the "closure" we expect funerals to provide, well-meaning friends and neighbors lovingly kept us well stocked with cards, food, and visits.

What I Learned

This period in my grief journey taught me some truths I feel blessed to have learned and to share.

1. When faced with a tragedy, what a person needs the most is your quiet and patient presence. Those who sat beside me, hugged me, and listened (if I wanted to talk) were the BEST!
2. DON'T tell a grieving person, "Time will heal." When death rips a loved one from you, the pain is unbearable. The phrase "time will heal" is trite and overused. So many people said it; I got sick to my stomach every time I heard it. I did not care WHEN or IF time would heal me; I just wanted to endure the moment I was experiencing. I love this quote by Rose Kennedy: *"It has been said that time heals all wounds. I don't agree. The wounds remain. Time - the mind, protecting its sanity - covers them with some scar tissue and the pain lessens, but it is never gone."*—Rose Kennedy
3. It is OK to say the dead person's name; in fact, it REASSURES the grieving parent that friends and family will remember their loved one. What a tremendous comfort!
4. It is wonderful to hear you will be in someone's thoughts. But it helped me more when friends or family prayed with me. Prayer comforted me and helped speed up my healing (which I will elaborate on in the next chapter).
5. The weeks following a tragedy are not the time to

expound your views on theology (unless you are the minister of the bereaved). We had some well-meaning church members who sent their friends (whom we had never met) to our house to share their views on life after death. Unfortunately, their views differed from what I believed, and the entire visit left me feeling sad and uncomfortable.

6. Finally, LIFE AROUND YOU MUST GO ON! Our daughter Amy went back to the university. I returned to teaching, and I forced myself to keep up with my exercise regimen. I had to "pretend" to enjoy being around others, even when I just wanted to be alone. Fortunately, I still prayed and received much comfort and healing through that very open line of communication. I am so grateful I was not angry with God… what an empowering and healing gift.

Back to Work

I quit teaching at SCS, only for two-and-a-half weeks; then, I went back to work. The first day back, my students and co-workers deluged me with smiles, hugs, and tears. What an emotional re-entry! It was still raining. Honestly, I don't remember driving to work or driving home. I am not sure what my mind was doing.

Thank you, God, for keeping me safe while driving.

Another Rainbow

Driving home a few days after returning to work, it stunned me to see a partial but vibrant rainbow in the sky. As I turned on the same road where I had witnessed the spectacular rainbow the day before Bart died, I saw ANOTHER one. It was different because it was a FULL rainbow from one side of the horizon to the other, right over our house. This time, I did not pull over to appreciate it. I wondered if this was a trick God was playing on me. Was this rainbow meant to encourage me? If so, what did it mean?

A few weeks later, our minister called and asked if I had time to come by for a visit. I met with him at our church, and he asked me if I had questions or things I needed to talk about. I quickly remembered the rainbow and said, "Yes, I have a question."

I asked him what he thought the second rainbow could mean, and I was brutally honest about how confused I felt when I saw it.

After many seconds of silence, he explained perhaps it was God's way of letting me know Bart was now complete. Just as the second rainbow was entirely complete, everything He created Bart to do, be, and accomplish was now finished. He was where he was meant to be, doing everything God intended!

I never see a rainbow without thinking Bart is happy, fulfilled, and joyfully doing what he was designed for all along....

Life Goes On

Life must go on.

Amy returned to the University of Texas in Austin. She attempted to focus on her schoolwork and her sorority's activities. John and I made several trips to Austin. The first one, soon after Bart died, was to attend parents' weekend. Amy loved the friends she had made at UT and was eager for us to meet their parents.

Life needed to go on for her, too. To keep things moving forward in her life and to spend quality time with our daughter, we attended numerous parties and dinners. I remember how genuinely her friends and their parents tried to visit with us and make us feel welcome. They cautiously walked that "line" of being friendly and not knowing what to say.

I felt like I lived in two worlds: the world of the present and the world of deep thought and gut-wrenching emotion where no one could enter.

I felt the same way when we got together with family and friends. John has an older brother and a younger sister. We all lived in Fort Worth, and they also had children. There were still Sunday get-togethers, birthday celebrations, anniversaries, and holidays. I often wondered, "How can everyone possibly be this happy and continue to LIVE their lives? Don't they understand our misery and how much we hurt?"

PART THREE: THE PUZZLE

" *If you then, being evil, know how to give good gifts to your children, how much more will your Father who is in heaven give good things to those who ask Him!* "

—Matthew 7:11 (NKJV)

TREASURE #7: GIFT OF THE MOVING CLOUD

"And the Lord went before them by day in a pillar of cloud to lead the way, and by night in a pillar of fire to give them light, so as to go by day and night."
—Exodus 13:21 (NKJV)

How Did I Get Here?

I n the fight-or-flight plethora of choices we experience when we feel threatened, scared, or when facing acute stress, I am, for sure, a flight risk.

It's hard for me to share my feelings with others. So, it was easier to decide I would not be coming back to teach. I realized, however, I would need to visit my students, friends, and the staff.

They were all unconditionally supportive of any decision I made, so I believe it was divine intervention leading me to change my mind and return to full-time teaching.

The first week or so after I returned, I remembered nothing about the drive there... it was as if a cloud hovered over me, directing my path. I did not remember the turns I had made or what I had seen on the way. Arriving at school in a fog, I did my best to interact with my students and their parents, write lesson plans, and keep current with their grades.

The fog would return on my way home. One day I was driving home, and I remember looking to my left just in time to see an elderly lady run a stop sign. I suddenly stepped on my brakes as she sped past me, not realizing she did not have the right of way. My emotions were so numb I did not even get upset with her. Sadly, I did not feel relief when she didn't plow into the driver's side of my car.

God's Timing

Two weeks before Bart's accident, one of my student's parents had brought a beautifully illustrated book for me to read to the class. I had so enjoyed reading the first few pages of *Someday Heaven*, by Larry Libby. It describes God's promises to us of eternal life using Scripture through meaningful analogies and captivating stories. The beautiful and meaningful illustrations helped get the points across.

Every time I read aloud from this book, ALL the students would stop what they were doing, listen intently, and wait for me to walk past their desks to show them the beautiful illustrations.

When I returned to teaching, they begged me to continue reading the book. Many times I had to ask a student to finish reading the segment because my tears blurred the words on the pages. After reading as much as time allowed, the students raised their hands to ask questions springboarding us into meaningful Bible-based discussions on:

- Is heaven real?
- How do we know we are going there?
- Will we see loved ones and people we have known in heaven?
- What will we do there?

Bringing life to books through reading aloud was a passion instilled in me by my fourth-grade teacher. Was it possible God was calling me through these circumstances with this book to keep me in His "classroom"?

Perhaps I was never meant to teach physically blind children as I had thought as a teenager, but instead to lead young people closer to faith in God through Christ by honestly and painfully sharing my real-life experiences. Was the Holy Spirit using my experiences and this book to help "cure" spiritual blindness?

As I continued to teach sixth, seventh, and eighth graders, it became my mission to read *Someday Heaven* aloud to every class. The last page of this book has a prayer of acceptance that invites the readers to silently pray. Many students have shared with me their joy in accepting Christ and being baptized in faith after listening to this book.

Perhaps their precious hearts were more open to heaven's possibilities because of the real-life stories I shared about Bart and why I am so confident he lives in heaven!

Seeing the Holy Spirit work through this book inspired me

to write *Tragedy's Treasures*! Just like *Someday Heaven*, I pray it nudges readers closer to Christ and heaven's door!

Cloud Movers

Clouds of grief overshadowed me at the weirdest times. One minute I was tending to everyday activities, and the next minute a paralyzing heaviness would press down on my body and spirit.

This suffocating "cloud" visited me one Saturday as I entered a dry-cleaning store to drop off some clothes.

Since I had not been hungry and probably had not eaten breakfast, the smells from the Subway restaurant next door to the dry cleaners lured me in. I heard a Christian radio station playing music, and I always enjoyed visiting with the beautiful African-American lady who owned the store. She was always smiling and friendly, and she had the most welcoming aura about her.

We exchanged greetings, visited briefly, and I returned to my car. Before I even got to my car, a quiet voice whispered, "Go back in there and ask her to pray for you!"

Being the stoic, "I can handle this," kind of person, I DID NOT WANT TO OBEY!

Since the oppressive cloud of sadness was still hovering, I hesitantly walked back in.

Other than me, no other customers were in her store, so through my tears, I shared with her why I had come back in. After listening intently, she invited me into the back part of Subway, took my hands, and prayed with me.

This experience was the first, but not the last time I felt the grief cloud move away.

The lady's name is Valerie, and I soon learned she was

looking for a church to attend. I invited her to mine, she visited, and it was a fit!

Prayer is SO powerful. One of the treasures I have opened is learning how powerful it is to pray for someone who is hurting.

PRAYER IS A "CLOUD MOVER."

TREASURE #8: GIFT OF REMEMBERING

"Those who sow in tears
Shall reap in joy."
—Psalm 126:5 (NKJV)

Memories of Bart

Memories are tricky. They can cut like a knife, but they also keep our loved ones alive in our hearts and minds.

Even now, decades later, I sometimes awaken with the hospital scene replaying in my mind, cutting into my heart, and reminding me how much I miss my son. There are still moments when an eerie warmth fills my heart and radiates out through my body, my eyes fill with tears, and I can almost physically feel Bart's presence. To feel him so close and to experience "communication" is a gift I do not take lightly.

The majority of Bart's sixteen years were devoted to his friends, his faith, and golf. I place friends first; he was, after all, a "normal" teenage boy. He didn't talk much about his faith, but after his death, the stories his friends poured out to me supported his faith in action. His dedication and commitment to the game of golf were apparent to all who knew him.

Bart's golf coach, Herb Stephens, died in 2019. Every year before that, he made sure all the high school golfers, their parents, and coaches who came to the annual Bart Granger Memorial learned about Bart's personality, talent, and character. John and I still attend each tournament and speak at the opening and closing.

Herb Stephens

A Story Shared

Herb shared a funny story about a day they canceled school due to snow and ice. I remember Bart talked me into taking him to the school because Coach was there, and they had an indoor net he could hit balls into, as well as an AstroTurf-covered putting green he could use.

The holes cut in the concrete were smaller than regulation holes on real greens. The coach did this on purpose; if the golfers could make putts into a smaller hole, how much easier it would be to make their putts during tournaments.

We slipped and slid all the way there, and I instructed him to call me when he was ready to come home. I busied myself at home, making homemade vegetable soup for dinner as I waited for the call. Several times during the day, I spoke to Coach to make sure it was okay for Bart to be there. He assured me they were doing just fine.

I didn't know it at the time, but Bart had called his coach early that morning asking if he would go to the school so he could come and practice.

Bart practiced in the basement while Coach graded papers upstairs in his office. Down a flight of stairs below the classroom, he could hear Bart hitting balls. If it got too quiet, Coach knew he was on the way up to "check on" his coach. "I would have been disappointed if he hadn't come up," Coach Stephens said. When he came in, Coach stopped working, and they would talk.

He loved practicing and being around his coach. I finally got a call late in the afternoon from Coach that he was bringing Bart home. I knew he could have used the day to get more done, especially since Bart had been stuck to him like glue. So, when he dropped Bart off, I met him at his truck with some homemade soup for his dinner.

The Bart Granger Memorial Golf Tournament

Since Bart's funeral, the annual high-school boys' golf tournament in Fort Worth, Texas, has been The Bart Granger Memorial. Little did we know on that painful day we lost him, that decades later, the tournament would still attract fifty teams of the best male high school golfers from Texas. Some teams would even come from out of state!

Coach Stephens always had a vision of hosting the largest

and most prestigious high school golf tournament in America. He said, "That's what my kids deserve."

To do this, he arranged with the Pecan Valley golf course in Ft. Worth, Texas, to block off their two courses for Friday and most of Saturday from paying customers. The high school golfers would play thirty-six holes on Friday (both courses) and eighteen holes on Saturday.

Using Friday's scores, the best teams would play on the "river" course on Saturday. The rest would play the "hills" course. This is where their physical and mental conditioning mattered. The boys couldn't ride in carts or use pushcarts. They walked, played, and carried their bags for thirty-six holes on Friday and eighteen on Saturday. Since 1998, rules have relaxed, and they may use pushcarts.

To pay for the green fees and the use of the course, a minimum of fifty school teams each paid their entry fees and their expenses. The first year, forty-seven teams signed up, and four cancelled.

In September 1997, three weeks before Bart's accident, fifty teams played. Along with teammates Adam Rubinson, Brian Williams, Bradley Boyd, and John Cockrell, Paschal WON the fifty-four-hole golf tournament with a total combined score of 874. Bart had the lowest scores of 72-69-73. Adam Rubinson was second with 72-72-71.

The following quote appeared in an article on high school golf in 2009 and still describes the impact of this prestigious tournament.

"The annual Bart Granger Memorial Tournament has a reputation, one it deserves. The two-day event is the largest high school golf tournament in the country, and arguably one of the most prestigious. Fort Worth Paschal High School hosts the tournament each year. The event is named after a former PHS golfer who was killed in a car accident in 1997. The tournament has ballooned into a field of more than 50 teams and over 250 players from across all classes and several states."[1]

Our family feels humbled and honored that we are still involved because the Bart Granger Memorial is such a prominent and prestigious tournament these many years later.

After he died, many coaches, friends, and parents of players contributed to a scholarship in his honor. For many years the scholarship fund gave money to young men wanting to play golf in college. A committee chose the recipients based on their character, hard work, and love of the game of golf. Adam Rubinson, Bart's friend and teammate, received the first scholarship in 1998.

It meant everything to Bart to be on the Paschal Golf team. Herb Stephens said,

"Bart embodied what Paschal golf is all about. This tournament is first class all the way in his honor. Everything I had hoped would happen did happen that year. Bart witnessed the growth, and it became more prestigious after he died."

The Team Plays On

After Bart died, the team chose to play the rest of their fall tournaments with a four-man team instead of five, leaving the second spot open in honor of Bart. In high school golf tournaments, the player's highest score out of the five gets dropped from the team total.

So, playing with only four players meant each of the four players' scores would count, leaving no room for error. Coach never asked the Paschal team to dedicate any tournament to Bart, but they committed every practice to him for the rest of the year.

The first match his team played after his death was in Arlington, Texas. The thunderstorms were so intense they stopped the tournament. Coach remembered me telling him, "I guess Bart didn't want you to play today!"

The next tournament on the schedule was in College Station, Texas. A&M Consolidated High School hosted the tournament. Once again, the team left the second spot open for Bart, and once again, it rained!

The first day it rained softly but with no lightning. So, the boys finished playing and wound up in third place after eighteen holes. They began playing on day two, and it got colder, wetter, and began to sleet.

Because of the weather, the tournament ended after nine holes. In those nine holes, Paschal went from third to first. They won the tournament!

As all the cold, wet players, parents, and coaches watched, Coach Danny Hayes presented the trophies to Bart's teammates and Coach Stephens, and $250 for the Bart Granger Scholarship. He had collected fifty dollars from each of his five players to add to the scholarship fund. All the teams knew about Bart's accident. Coach Hayes cried through the presentations, as did everyone else.

A Trip to Regionals and State

Spring always signals a new beginning, so a fifth player and a close friend to Bart, George Lewis, joined the roster for the five upcoming tournaments. The boys continued to play well and hard all year. They won their district competition and went on to win the regional championship in Lubbock, Texas.

I went to Lubbock to watch the boys and support their efforts. Bart had been so close to all the golf team members, and it inspired me to watch their talent and drive.

I remember standing at the edge of one of the greens and seeing a young man from another school storm off the green after missing his putt and fling his club at his golf bag. He crouched down head in his hands, staring at the ground. I knew he was having a serious talk with himself about missing his putts.

When I knew the others had finished putting, I walked over to him, put my hand on his shoulder, and told him my name and why I was there. His demeanor changed as his anger melted, and he began to listen attentively. I don't remember all I said to him, but it involved not being so hard on himself and being thankful he could be there on that day to play in the tournament.

He remembered perfectly what I said to him, because his mother, a freelance writer, submitted a story about his experiences to *Chicken Soup for the Golfer's Soul.*

Several months later, a box arrived on my front porch. I opened it to find a copy of the book with a personal note from his mom. Her letter explained how her son had shared our conversation with her. What he shared fueled her story describing Bart's death. She wrote of the profound impact our conversation had on her son's attitude about himself and his golf game. I treasure the book and her note!

———————

Because of their performance in Lubbock, Paschal's golf team played in the State playoffs in Austin, Texas. Bart's dad and I both went to cheer for them.

I always felt comforted being around the people Bart loved so much. But his father's pain magnified as he watched his son's teammates compete, knowing Bart could not play.

The boys finished fifth in the state competition. Coach Stephens said,

"This was the first tournament where the emotion of not having Bart got to the team. They had played so well, so hard all year on an emotional high that ran out in Austin."

TREASURE #9: THE GIFT OF KNOWING

"Behold, children are a heritage from the Lord,
The fruit of the womb is a reward."
— Psalm 127:3 (NKJV)

Learning More About Bart

How well do we really know our children? When we become parents and mature adults, do inner thoughts about our childhood experiences lurk in our memories, hoping to stay hidden? Don't we all have failures, faults, and sins, confessed or not, we don't want to be exposed?

In the days and weeks following Bart's death, his closest friends spent hours at our home, sharing stories of their experiences with him. Some were funny, some were surprising, and some were even alarming. Maybe it made them feel his memory would stay vibrant longer if they revealed his secrets to me.

Regardless of their motivation, I learned more about his

humor, spunkiness, and his ability to listen to his friends. Amazed at how many friends he had, both male and female, I learned that girls would frequently call him at night (when he should have been studying/sleeping) to get his advice on friendship or relationship issues.

His golfing friends admitted how much money he had won in their contests on the putting greens. Cameron, a close friend who was also a passenger in the truck the day of the accident, took forty dollars he owed Bart from bets won and threw it in the water on the thirteenth hole at Colonial Country Club.

Another friend, Bradley, set a Dr. Pepper can on a stump by the water on the same golf hole. Bart drank too many of them. Amazingly, the can sat there for almost three weeks, reminding us all of his personality.

The Good and the Bad

Even knowing more about his faults and "sins" was comforting. The stories his friends shared sparked the flames that have helped to keep him alive in my heart and mind.

However, it was not as gratifying finding the cans of chewing tobacco in his underwear drawer or the magazines under his bed.

When I finally made myself enter his room, Bart's smells slapped me: the faint scent of his cologne, the scent of the stuffed animals he still had on his bed, and the smell of his sweaty, dirty clothes stuffed in black garbage bags in his closet.

We required him to do his laundry. I suspected he had been wearing the same clothes for much too long. I already knew he slept on top of his bedspread with his clothes on so he could sleep longer instead of making his bed. No wonder the soft, brown, flattened teddy bear I had given him when he was born smelled so much like him.

After his death, I gave the bear to his girlfriend. They met at driver-education classes. Kelly went to school in Arlington, Texas, but this didn't deter them from long phone conversations and time spent together at each other's respective homes. We quickly fell in love with her, and Bart loved her parents' humor and acceptance. Her dad is still a prominent dentist in Arlington. I reaped the rewards of his work ethic and talent in dentistry for several years after Bart's death. Kelly eventually gave Bart's bear back to me. It now lives with my grandchildren.

Bart Turns Sixteen

After his birthday in March 1997, he passed his driver's license test. Before his test, he enjoyed practicing his driving with us in the car. Confident he knew how to drive safely and navigate through town, we permitted him to drive to his girl-friend's house. He wasn't used to driving such a long distance, so we asked him to call us when he arrived and again when he started home.

About the time he was due to return, I heard a loud and abrasive crunch! I ran into the garage only to see a dented left front corner of the car and the scraped-up edge of the garage. Bart did not look hurt, but he was lying on the garage floor with his hands over his face in dismay.

He had two more unfortunate driving experiences he probably would not want me to share. But, maybe his experiences will remind young, newbie drivers of the pitfalls lurking in their newfound independence.

The second mistake happened on the way to East Texas. His dad and I accepted an invitation to spend the weekend at John's boss's lake house to fish, enjoy the piney woods, and relax.

After John had finished work, we stopped in Dallas to eat dinner and began our drive. Bart asked to drive, but it was getting late and dark. Having taught school all week, I was almost asleep in the back seat when the car swerved into the next lane before pulling over to stop.

Fortunately for all of us, we were the only ones on the highway, because Bart had fallen asleep while driving.

He didn't take his actions lightly. He loved to go fishing, and his anticipation of enjoying the weekend now included the somber realization of what he had done and what could have happened.

Three Strikes

His dad grounded him from driving for several months for the third infraction (Bart's sister thought the punishment exceeded the crime, but in hindsight, I am not so sure).

Since his sister, Amy, was attending the University of Texas, we bought her a car more worthy of traveling on the highway. Bart inherited her old car, an Acura with automatic seat belts. It was a good car for driving back and forth to high school and for driving to Arlington to see his girlfriend.

But one morning after Bart had driven to school, I received a call from a man asking me if I was Bart's mom. I didn't recognize his voice, but he explained the reason for his call.

Seeing Bart speeding down his street, he had written down his driver's license plate number. I don't remember asking how he got our phone number because too many thoughts and questions were crowding the logic right out of my brain.

I was thinking, "How could this man know what kind of driver my son is, and what business is it of his?" He explained he hoped his call would slow Bart down and prevent an accident in his future. I thanked him for calling, and after I had more time to think about it, I appreciated his call. His dad and I took away his driving privileges for six months but reduced the "sentence" to three for good behavior.

My mother had been a compulsive worrier. I grew up seeing the stress she put on herself (and on me), so I made every effort NOT to worry. Perhaps I went too far, not realizing the hazards.

We tried to help Bart understand he could injure himself and others by driving too fast or too recklessly. But I never even thought about discussing how to be a safe passenger in someone else's car.

PART FOUR: THE LIVING

"You, Lord, keep my lamp burning;
my God turns my darkness into light."
—Psalm 18:28 (NIV)

TREASURE #10: GIFT OF FEARLESS FREEDOMS

"For I, the Lord your God, will hold your right hand,
Saying to you,
Fear not, I will help you."
—Isaiah 41:13 (NKJV)

Unexpected Gifts

In the days, weeks, and months following my son's death, I had trouble putting one foot in front of the other. The pain of losing Bart paralyzed my thoughts, my feelings, and my energy.

But God's plan for me did not include staying immobilized and numb. He helped me keep going. Looking back, I realize my personality began to change, and my faith grew as I learned to treasure life again.

There were unexpected gifts along the way. I learned to feel freedoms that continue to build upon each other. Some "freedoms" were almost immediate:

1. Freedom to fail
2. Freedom to say "No"
3. Freedom to face my fears and insecurities
4. Freedom to nurture myself

An Only Child

Soon after her brother died, Amy said, "Oh No, now I am an only child!"

As if her current situation wasn't traumatic enough, she began to consider how his death would impact the rest of her life. She had not only lost a brother but was now left alone with the sole responsibility of taking care of aging parents. Since I am an only child, I felt her pain!

Plenty of research exists on the personality traits of only children and how being an only child affects adult relationships. If spoiled and overprotected, they may not be as self-confident as children who learn at an early age that it is okay to fail.

My parents did not spoil me in the manner of getting extra materialistic things. I was, however, shielded from emotional stress when things did not turn out as planned. They tried to make my road easier by hiding the everyday stresses of life. I never saw my parents argue, only the after-effects of sulky silence until the problems went away.

Not having brothers and sisters to stand up to, confront, or argue with put me at a disadvantage. That, coupled with not seeing my parents disagree and work through problems to come out stronger on the other side, severely limited my ability to TALK about stress and made me hesitant to stand up for myself.

Thankfully, my parents worked hard to make sure we lived in a neighborhood where I could attend public school to get a good education. We moved to a new area when I started junior high (this so dates me, because now we call it middle school).

Moving to a new school in a new neighborhood made me sad and uncomfortable. Leaving the comfort of my home and my friends was not my choice. But my parents knew it would be a safer and happier environment.

It didn't take long for me to appreciate not having to ride the school bus. I had been bullied and made fun of on the bus in our old neighborhood. My new school was closer to home and much newer and more modern.

It felt intimidating not having brothers or sisters to help pave the way for me socially in my new school. I found comfort in making two or three close friends, but even in high school, being a part of the "in-group" was not in my DNA.

Only children may be more introverted than those with siblings because of all the time they spend alone. It still challenges me to be in a large group of people I don't know well. I am more relaxed in a small group, especially if I share their interests or abilities.

On the positive side, being alone has always been restorative, even more since Bart's death. I have learned I can think, meditate, and write to center my thoughts and feelings on what I feel is essential and healing.

Freedom to Fail

In high school, I spent most of my time and attention studying to make good grades. I got used to meeting the high expectations set by my parents in academics, friendship choices, and being responsible and trustworthy. Since only children spend so much time with grown-ups, they may be expected to act more "adult."

Perhaps my perfectionist tendencies and being critical of myself stemmed from not wanting to make mistakes as a young child. I missed the learning lessons on how to fail, get back up, and move forward even stronger. This fearless freedom grew after my son died.

Freedom to Say No

I learned to say, "No," through becoming a grief recovery class dropout. So many friends lovingly suggested attending a grief-recovery class might help, and one was starting at our church. Fighting my "wanting to be alone" tendencies, I called to reserve my spot.

Two other women in our group had lost children under different and tragic circumstances. One, a family practice doctor's wife, had been on a family winter ski trip when their young daughter died while sledding. The saucer-shaped sled slammed into a pole. Even though her dad was a doctor, there was nothing they could do to save her.

The other woman's story was familiar to me because her children went to the school where I taught. Two of her children had been in an elevator when the youngest got trapped. Somehow the door closed and crushed him while his sister watched. A few years later, his sister was in my sixth-grade class.

In our first grief class, we all introduced ourselves and shared why we had come. I was okay with that.

Then the teacher asked us to give more details about how we FELT. I suddenly felt claustrophobic.

As the facilitator circled behind us, touching our shoulders when it was time for us to share, I had a powerful urge to jump up and run away. To me, she was invading my space, and I felt very uncomfortable. Staying in my seat until the end of the class was excruciating. I never went back. My prayer and devotional time and my time with my students became my grief recovery "class."

Through this experience, I learned if friends or relatives invited me to lunch or a social function I did not wish to attend, saying, "No, thank you," or "No, but thank you for asking," was acceptable.

They were trying to help get me out in the world, and I appreciated their concern. What a relief to learn that I controlled my activities. If I chose not to participate, I wouldn't hurt anyone's feelings. The more I bowed out, the easier it became.

Freedom to Face Fears

Isn't it interesting how we all are fearful of something? Maybe we fear heights, snakes, confining spaces, bees, spiders, or going on airplanes.

Falling face down on an open-grate floor heater at two years old and having minor burns on my face and hands, carved a fear of fire into me. Seeing fire scenes in movies or on television almost makes me nauseous. When I know a fire scene is impending, I cover my eyes. Watching fire breathers is not my live entertainment of choice!

My experiences with mosquito bites have made me fearful of bees, wasps, and yellow jackets. As a child, a mosquito bite would cause swollen welts that would crust over and ooze. A bite on an elbow or ankle sometimes caused severe swelling. As I got older, this continued to be painful and inconvenient, especially when I began following John around golf courses to watch him practice or play. I remember hobbling around from hole-to-hole with an ankle twice its normal size!

By the time Bart began playing in tournaments, I always kept a can of insect repellant nearby. Fortunately, a bee has never stung me. Based on the amount of swelling caused by mosquitos, who knows what would happen if a bee stung me?

Just days after our son died, John and I went to the golf course to get some fresh air so he could hit practice balls. The practice area has grassy knolls built up where several men or women can safely hit towards golf-flag targets. Practice sand traps are off to one side to provide practice with "around the green" skills.

Even in October, it is still warm in Texas, but the leaves on the massive trees were already turning their expected colors of vibrant reds, cheery oranges, and golden yellows. Stretched out on the grass behind him to see where his balls were landing added some peace to my thoughts and emotions.

My peace disappeared when a yellow jacket flew right past my face and landed on the ground about six inches from me. My attitude was abnormal. I said, "Come on, big boy.

Give it your best shot. You can't hurt me any worse than I hurt right now!"

Ever since that day on the course, if a bee comes too close, I wait for it to leave or gently shoo it away.

Another fear I have faced is claustrophobia. To battle my fear of closed-in spaces, I have learned to avoid elevators by using escalators or taking the stairs.

We often waited until the crowds thinned out before leaving a movie, sporting event, or a concert. ALWAYS asking for an aisle seat on an airplane made it more comfortable to fly. John would graciously agree to be sandwiched into a middle seat just so the aisle seat would be available for me.

Early in our marriage, we had gone to a movie with friends. After buying our tickets and going inside, the crowds began pushing us toward the snack bar. More people kept coming until we had little or no space around us.

A claustrophobic, panicky feeling began to suffocate me as I pushed my way through the crowd toward the theatre's entrance. I could not wait to get outside, where there was room to breathe and space to move. Once the theatre personnel let the crowds enter the movie room, I came back and tried to settle down to watch the show.

I still have my fear of tight spaces. The aisle seat on an airplane is still my favorite, but I can now sit in the middle or window seat if I have to.

Maybe losing Bart made me bullet-proof. Physical pain still hurts. Stress and worries still peak through. Watching my aging parents die and being responsible for their funerals was sad, stressful, and draining. I miss them very much. But I am not sure anything I have experienced has hurt me as much as seeing my son unconscious and knowing he was brain dead.

Nurturing Myself

Maybe it was the era I grew up in that led me to try to make everyone around me happy. In times of deep sorrow and piercing grief pains, the body reacts physically, emotionally, and mentally.

My doctor and friends kept asking me, "Are you having trouble sleeping?"

My response was, "No, not at all; my problem is waking up!"

Sleeping through the night was much easier than opening my eyes and facing reality. First, the excruciating anguish hit me that Bart was dead. Next came the tedious lists in my brain of the day's activities and the people needing my attention.

Eating was not a priority. It took several weeks for me to get any amount of appetite back. As a result, others worried about how thin I became.

Wanting to make everyone around me feel better made it hard for me to cry and mourn. I didn't want anyone to see me hurting. Perhaps I was afraid if I cried, I might not stop.

In the years since Bart's death, I continue to learn my cup needs filling before I can give to others.

How do I nurture myself? What works for me?

- starting the day with Christ in prayer and with a Bible devotional (my favorite is a website called Our Daily Bread)
- drinking more water and eating fresh food (limiting everything white: sugar, flour, milk, starchy foods)

- eating more vegetables and foods from plants
- exercising (biking, hiking, and yoga)
- writing/journaling
- using essential oils for relaxation, stress relief, and health.

**Disclaimer: I do not always meet these goals. It is still a challenge to nurture myself. But my radar is now much more sensitive to taking care of ME and of doing the necessary things to restore my physical, emotional, mental, and spiritual needs.*

TREASURE #11: GIFT OF SHARING

"Call upon Me in the day of trouble.
I will deliver you, and you shall glorify Me."
— Psalm 50:15 (NKJV)

Sharing Leads to Healing

There are universal events and unexpected life changes we all share. All of us experience illnesses, either our own or someone else's. Grandparents, relatives, friends, and parents may die. We all face disappointments relating to our jobs, our marriages, our friends, etc.

Tragically, many parents have lost children through illness, accidents, or even suicide.

How can we be certain God understands how we feel when our child dies? We can look to Jesus for the answer.

In John 11, the Bible says Jesus traveled to Bethany (even though His trip there put Him in danger), because He heard his friend, Lazarus, had died. When he arrived, Lazarus had been in the tomb for four days. He found Mary, Martha, and their Jewish friends weeping.

> *"Therefore, when Jesus saw her weeping, and the*
> *Jews who came with her weeping, He groaned in*
> *the spirit and was troubled. And He said, "Where*
> *have you laid him?"*
> *They said to Him, "Lord, come and see."*
> ***Jesus wept.*** *Then the Jews said, "See how*
> *He loved him!"*
> *And some of them said, "Could not this Man, who*
> *opened the eyes of the blind, also have kept this*
> *man from dying?"* —John 11:33-37 (NKJV)

When Jesus came to his tomb, he asked them to remove the stone at the entrance.

> *"Then they took away the stone from the place where*
> *the dead man was lying. And Jesus lifted up His*
> *eyes and said, "Father, I thank You that You have*
> *heard Me. And I know that You always hear Me,*
> *but because of the people who are standing by I*
> *said this, that they may believe that You sent Me."*
> *Now when He had said these things, He cried with*
> *a loud voice, "Lazarus, come forth!" And he who*
> *had died came out bound hand and foot with*
> *graveclothes, and his face was wrapped with a*
> *cloth. Jesus said to them, "Loose him, and let him*
> *go."* —John 11:41-44 (NKJV)

Because Jesus **wept** when he got to Lazarus, even though He knew He could raise him back to life, we know God loves us and understands our heartache when we grieve. In His love, power, and wisdom, He comforts and guides us through the whole process. We also know God is our Healer. He wants us to come out on the other side of tragedy stronger than before.

Just as Jesus prayed so his followers would hear him and believe God sent Him, maybe we should share our grief and experiences with others to strengthen their belief and help them in their journey.

Perhaps He knows that sharing leads to healing. Does our sharing make it easier to open God's gifts?

The dictionary defines sharing as "relating (a secret or experience, for example) to another or others."

How could God expect me, an introvert, to climb out of my box of misery to share my thoughts and feelings with others? For me, He led me in small steps.

When I decided to return to SCS and finish the year with my sixth graders, I was "set up," especially in Bible class, to share my thoughts and feelings as they related to the Bible. So, my first arena was the classroom.

God knew this non-denominational Christian school would be the perfect place for me because it was such a warm and nurturing place. As I came back the next year and the next, I reassured my students on the first day of school after introducing myself,

"Please don't get scared or embarrassed if I cry when talking about Bart. Only be alarmed if I pass out or throw up! Then you may go ask for help."

Staying in contact with several students has taught me how God used Bart's death to bring their faith to a much deeper and more tangible level.

Each successive year in the classroom showed me how sharing leads to healing and hope.

Sharing His Heart

One day, Bart's father and I received a letter addressed to both of us. It was from Life Gift, the donor organization, which made it so much less painful to donate Bart's organs… at least the ones they could use and find donors for.

The letter stated the man who received Bart's heart wanted to meet us. He had already sent one letter to us. Either I read it and didn't comprehend, accidentally threw it away, or we never received it.

I shared the letter with John and Amy, and we agreed we would call the family. Talking to them in person was painful and uncomfortable. It was the second major event that drew me out of my box.

What a story!

In our first phone conversation, the man confirmed he had mailed a letter to us to introduce himself and thank us for giving him a second chance at life. Through his soft tone of voice and gentle words of sympathy, he came across as genuine and humble.

The one thing I remember from our family's discussion before donating Bart's organs was when Amy said,

"I hope a young person gets his heart."

That didn't happen.

Paul Meadows was seventy. He and his wife, Helen, lived thirty miles from our home in Dallas, Texas. It seemed vital to him for us to meet in person, so John, Amy, and I drove to Dallas to meet them. The drive there was pensive and quiet; we were all lost in our thoughts and insecurities about what was ahead.

Parking on the street in front of their house, climbing out of the car, and walking up their long sidewalk to ring the doorbell was nerve-racking.

IF ANYONE OF THE THREE OF US HAD SAID, "LET'S GO HOME," WE PROBABLY WOULD HAVE RACED EACH OTHER TO THE CAR. FOR ME, THE FEELINGS NOT ALREADY NUMBED BY BART'S DEATH SENT COLD BUTTERFLIES INTO MY STOMACH.

Meeting Mr. Meadows

Both Paul and Helen answered the doorbell and graciously invited us in. Helen was a bit more reserved than Paul as they led us into their beautiful living room. They sat in chairs close to each other, and all three of us sat on a long couch facing them. Paul did most of the talking about what he remembered.

He humbly described what he went through. Right off the bat, Paul wanted us to know how grateful he was to us for donating our son's heart, and how sad it made him Bart had died.

He explained the doctors had done all they could do for him. His heart was failing. "I would not have left the hospital without a new heart," Paul explained. "Because of my age, they did not want to put me on the donor list. But because of my physical strength outside of my heart issues and our willingness and ability to pay for the lengthy and expensive process following the transplant, they added me to the recipient list."

The details of how many factors there are in matching donors with their recipients fascinated all three of us. Even though our families lived only thirty miles apart, our two cities were in different transplant "zones." When Bart's heart became available, protocol required them to exhaust the needs in our area before moving on to other regions. Bart had an unusual blood type (AB positive), which perfectly matched Paul's type.

Other factors to be considered are:

1. Blood and tissue type
2. Size of the heart
3. Medical urgency of the patient's illness
4. Time already spent on the waiting list
5. Geographical distance between donor and recipient[1]

Paul added, "Besides the blood type, the cavity's size the heart fits into had to match, and ours did."

Paul's wife, Helen, who had been quietly listening, asked if she could share what happened before Bart's accident. After three bypasses, Paul's heart was still out of rhythm. On September 5, the doctors shocked his heart eleven times in a row, and it began to beat again. Then, he had a "code blue" on the September 7. Still in the hospital, he was told on the October 1, he had five blood clots, and things looked grim.

Next she shared what she saw on the second of October, eight days before Bart's accident.

She said, "I was sitting in a chair next to Paul's bed, trying to stay awake to watch him sleep. The room was quiet and dimly lit, so I dozed off. Someone or something moving awakened me. As I looked toward the door, I saw two white, shadowy figures standing at the end of Paul's bed. At first, I thought they were in his room because he might be dying, but that was not the case. I waited. They didn't speak, and in my heart, I knew Paul would be OK."

Sitting in Paul and Helen's living room, we learned the optimum time between removing the heart and transplanting it is four to five hours.

They shared with us at eleven p.m. on the tenth of October (the day of Bart's accident), the nurses came into their room to tell them they had found a match. Helen and her children stayed up all night to see the helicopter carrying Bart's heart land on the roof of their hospital in Dallas.

It arrived in the early hours of the morning of the eleventh, and their heart surgeon began performing the surgery at seven a.m.

After the surgery, the recovery nurse couldn't believe the reading from the monitor which measured the strength of Paul's new heartbeats. The normal is five, and his was reading 7.5!

Mountains and Valleys

Researching this grueling process the heart recipient goes through has opened my eyes to the mountains and valleys Paul experienced. He immediately began taking multiple drugs to keep his body from rejecting Bart's heart. Besides the terrific expense, many of these medications can have serious side effects.

The good news is immunosuppressant drugs control the rejection, but the bad news is they can reduce the strength of the body's immune system and its defenses against infection. Other medications include antibiotics, blood-pressure lowering drugs, and diuretics to reduce fluid buildup.

Some side effects are:
  high cholesterol
  swelling of feet, hands, abdomen, or face
  anxiety
  increased appetite
  tingling hands and feet
  bone disease
  increased blood sugar
  tremors (shaking)
  diarrhea
  kidney damage
  trouble sleeping
  gum overgrowth
  mood swings
  unwanted hair growth
  hair loss
  nausea
  vomiting
  headache
  sensitivity to the sun
  weight gain
  high blood pressure.

Long-term use of immunosuppression drugs may also cause specific forms of cancer, especially skin and lymph gland tumors.

Besides taking so many drugs, there are ten-to-twelve biopsies the first year in which the doctors take specimens of the heart muscle. Once a month, the patient gets a local anesthetic and a catheter is inserted into the heart through a vein in the neck. Using x-ray equipment, the doctor guides the catheter into the heart and removes tissue. This grueling process continues every year after the transplant as frequently as necessary to prevent rejection.

How long do heart recipients live? The longevity outlook is eighty-five percent for ONE YEAR, seventy-five percent for FIVE YEARS, and fifty to sixty percent live TEN YEARS (plus).

Until Paul received Bart's heart, they only placed recipients on the list if they were sixty-five years or younger. After his successful surgery and recovery, the Life Gift Organization changed its age restrictions for older adults to a "case-by-case" basis. His will to live, God's healing power, and Bart's heart made it possible!

⸻

So what was Paul, the man, like? He and Helen had a grown son and daughter. Their son worked in his father's business-consulting firm, Paul Meadows & Associates Inc. Their daughter was divorced and had a son her parents helped raise. So, Paul had been particularly close to his grandson.

At 70 years young, he continued to work as a consultant for hotels and resorts. His job required traveling, but he was not ready to stop working. Paul also became an advocate and public speaker for organ donation, sharing his story and all he had learned about Bart.

As we shared our family's history, we soon learned there

were several important dates and events we had in common, such as birthdays, anniversaries, etc.

On the way back to Fort Worth, my mind screamed out all the proofs of how God had turned our tragedy into something good…

> *"And we know that all things work together for good to those who love God, to those who are the called according to His purpose."* — Romans 8:28 (NKJV)

Post Heart Transplant

We didn't talk to Paul and Helen too much after that. He sent correspondence through the mail from time to time, and he would call occasionally. He called us after his biopsies to let us know his body was not rejecting "his heart,"and he was physically and emotionally stronger with each year that passed. He also shared cute stories about his grandson—the fun things they experienced together and the places they went.

Treasured Gifts

A few years after his transplant, I received a Christmas package in the mail from Paul. I quickly opened it and called to thank him. Helen answered the phone and told me the story behind the gift.

They were on vacation at the Biltmore Estate in Asheville, North Carolina. Paul was waiting for Helen to finish her shopping when he spotted some angels for sale. Not understanding why he was drawn to one angel, in particular, he announced he wanted to buy it for me. That surprised her because he usually left the gift buying to her.

Seeing this petite leaded glass angel holding a lyre was enough to melt my heart and make me cry. How could he have known I collect angels, and Bart often gave me a new one for my birthday and Christmas?

In May 2002, I invited Paul to come to Southwest Christian School to speak to our middle school chapel about organ donations. He shared with at least two hundred teenagers, teachers, and parents how Bart's organs, tissue, and skin had helped forty people.

You could have heard a pin drop in the gym when he explained since there are no nerves attached to the heart when it is transplanted, the "cap" of his heart was placed on top of the "cap" of Bart's. This is how the nerves of both hearts connect.

His honesty and compassion mesmerized the students, teachers, and parents. They asked the question, "How often do you think about having someone else's heart?" He answered, "Every minute of every day!"

West Nile Virus

Ten years after his transplant, Paul called one summer morning to tell us he had contracted West Nile Virus while pruning rose bushes in the corner of his backyard. As I listened intently to the amazing details, he explained he was now home from a two-week hospital stay. His words were, "Bart saved my life two times!"

After going to his doctor for fever, chills, aches, etc., they immediately hospitalized him. His condition rapidly declined until ALL of his body's systems shut down except HIS HEART. He was unconscious for about seven days, but his heart kept everything else alive. At the same time he was in the hospital, his wife, Helen, underwent heart bypass surgery. Recovery was slow but steady. They both recovered, and the doctors later told him he was the ONLY living heart recipient who had survived West Nile Virus.

Cancer

Then in 2009, Helen called to tell us Paul had cancer. She neglected to say where his cancer had started, probably because I forgot to ask. But by the time she called, he was terminal.

I remember telling her how sorry we were and asking her if there were anything we could do for her or Paul. In a weak and tired voice, she responded, "No, just pray." Paul died on August 6, 2009, twelve years after he received Bart's heart.

Leonard Paul Meadows, Jr.
June 14, 1927 - August 6, 2009
Dallas, Texas

My Regrets

Dear Paul,

Please forgive me for not coming to Dallas to see you before your death. Perhaps I thought I was too busy, or just maybe....

I couldn't face the idea of you dying. That meant Bart was dying again.

I wish I had told you what a remarkable and brave soldier you were and how blessed we were to have met you and your family.

Being the faith-filled man you were, I take comfort KNOWING you are now sharing stories with Bart. Medical science states heart transplant recipients don't assume the personality of their donors. Please don't let that stop you from sharing how you couldn't quit talking in the hospital... and how your sweet wife had to read the church bulletin aloud to you to make you stop.

I look forward to seeing you in "person" when I get there.

Love,

Karyn

Sharing My Heart

Two more sharing experiences, years apart, drew me out of my shell. One was speaking to the congregation of McKinney Bible Church, and the other was talking to SCS graduates. To each of these requests, my answer was, "Yes, not because I feel comfortable doing it, but because I don't want to waste a moment of my pain or Bart's life."

In January, only two years after Bart's death, our minister called and asked if he could talk to me for a few minutes. The thought crossed my mind that perhaps he was calling to "scold" me for walking out of the grief recovery class. The more he talked, the quieter I became.

I soon learned that was not the case. Our minister called to ask me to consider speaking at the Easter services—all four of them! What did he want me to say? Was it my experience of losing Bart and the hope in my heart? How could I possibly get up in front of the congregations of people without completely falling apart? What would I say? How would I hold myself together?

After thinking, praying, and agreeing, I began the hard work of writing the message. The parents and relatives of the young man who was driving when Bart died were members of our church. Thinking of their families sitting in the audience made it harder to decide which details to share!

His mother and I had attended the same women's church retreat. There we had private time to talk and pray together. She revealed her son had crawled out of the driver's window in the upside-down truck to walk to a house nearby for help. With broken bones, this was a feat. He called his mother, and she rushed to the scene.

She cautiously shared with me when she arrived, the paramedics were working on Bart. They told her they didn't think he would make it. She went to the ground, placed Bart's head in her lap, and talked to him, reassuring him he wasn't alone.

I am so grateful she prayed for him while the trained paramedics helped her son and the other young man, Cameron, who had been sitting in the middle of the truck's cab. More ambulances arrived. One delivered Cameron to Fort Worth Children's Hospital, and another transported Bart and the driver to Harris Hospital.

The driver of the truck sustained injuries to his spine ending his baseball scholarship dreams. Cameron walked down the aisle of the church on the day of Bart's funeral on crutches. He had a broken ankle, pelvis, and arm.

My talk for our church lasted fifteen minutes or so and was titled, "There Are No Accidents." Bart's dad, our daughter, my mother, and many of Bart's friends sat in the front rows to support me. They smiled and cried as they listened. By the end of my sharing, there were many others in the congregation also crying.

My second sharing experience took place at Southwest Christian School for a pre-graduation celebration. Their Senior Chapel was the final time the parents saw their kids in a school program before they graduated. Even more meaningful was the prayer time at the close of the program. Prayers lifted the families and the students to bless them and ask for God to prepare them to go out into the world and to equip them to be a light for Him.

Each year, the school invited a respected speaker to address the students, faculty, and parents. This year, they asked me! I taught this group in sixth grade the year Bart died. Remember the young man who went to the front of the classroom and asked his friends and classmates to pray for me? They had requested me, so how could I say, "No"?

Life is like a treasure hunt. Moving from one treasure to the next is sometimes painful, as unexpected circumstances are part of the journey.

If we can MOVE through the tragedies TRUSTING God to give us exactly what we need to put one foot in front of the other, the growth and changes we experience are inevitable.

Sharing leads to healing, and God can use our pain to encourage and inspire others.

TREASURE #12: GIFT OF SELF-DISCOVERY

"...for I know whom I have believed and am
persuaded that He is able
to keep what I have committed to Him until that Day."
— 2 Timothy 1:12 (NKJV)

So Many Changes

C hange has always been difficult for me. If furniture and decorations stayed in their spots for years, I would be happy. But, we all know when our lives take sudden and unexpected turns, our needs and wants change.

Changes in my personal life have included divorce, re-entry into the teaching world, caring for aging parents and my mother's sister until their deaths, marrying, and moving out of the town where I was born and lived for fifty-nine years.

WHEW! It seems much more dramatic writing about it than living it!

Aging Parents

Being an only child turns into an enormous challenge when parents age. My dad developed thyroid and lung cancer, sending him to heaven at eighty-one. We spent precious hours together towards the end of his life—listening, sharing, and caring.

The thirteenth hole at the Colonial golf course made a perfect place for the two of us to spend time together. We went on Monday because they closed the golf course for maintenance.

Trees and sloping banks outlined this small lake. Besides being Bart's favorite golf hole, he and my dad had spent many Mondays fishing and spending time together under the trees. They rarely caught any fish. They did make many sacred memories.

Knowing how to drive into the course through an open gate, we accessed the thirteenth hole. Sitting on the side of a small hill overlooking the green and the small lake separating the green from the tee box, we would share our thoughts and feelings. My dad seemed to be on a mission to share his life's story with me.

———

My dad served in the Navy at the end of WWII, and he had fascinating stories to tell. One story, in particular, showed me the great lengths he went to, even as a very young man in the Navy, to defend his honor.

He once requested a meeting with the commanding officer on his ship, the USS Crescent City, to set the record straight about being unjustly accused of making an error that put his shipmates in danger. I am ashamed to admit I did not write what he told me, so I have forgotten many of the important details.

I do remember my dad's superior officer thought he saw him make a mistake. He reprimanded my dad. Not wanting to argue with his superior, he went all the way to the TOP. As he explained to me, "They could have court-martialed me for even requesting the meeting with the captain of the ship. But I knew I was not in the wrong, and I wanted the record set straight."

On the day of his meeting, the ship's crew members lined up on each side of him to show their support as he walked up the ladder to meet with the captain. He also revealed he was more nervous about this meeting than he was about being a gunner on a naval ship in WWII. Fortunately, for him, the meeting was a success, and the captain cleared his name.

I also learned more about his other two marriages before he married my mom. Out of respect for my mom and her love for my dad, I will not reveal the details. However, his honesty inspired me, and I treasure everything he shared.

―――――

When his cancer advanced, we called hospice. For a few weeks, they came to his house to care for him. He became more stubborn each day about wanting to stay home rather than going to the hospital. My mother's biggest fear (other than losing him) was that he might die at home.

I convinced him he would get better care at the hospital and promised to stay in his room with him so he wouldn't be alone. He agreed, and we checked him in.

Keeping my promise, I spent two nights with him. The

first night was terrible. He was on morphine for pain, and he talked ALL night telling me many of the stories I had already heard. About the time I would doze off in the cold, hard recliner, he started talking again. The next day he slept more (go figure), but he never woke up enough to converse. That same night, about two hours after I put in earplugs to muffle the sounds of his snoring, the lights came on. A nurse was at his side, gently patting his arm. She quietly told me he had died. I knew she was telling me the truth because his snoring had stopped. Now I understood the importance of staying up all night the night before listening to him.

I would not trade anything for those last two nights with him.

My next life-changing hurdle was to persuade my mother to sell her home and move to an assisted living. Her health kept her from living alone. Just before Dad died, her doctors diagnosed her with Lewy Body Dementia. Her symptoms included a sleep behavior disorder where sufferers act out their dreams. She also experienced visual hallucinations, anxiety, depression, and slowness of movement.

Their house never went on the market. One of their dear friend's children wanted to buy it. We had an estate sale, found a place close to me she liked (sort of), and moved her to the first of two assisted living centers she would occupy.

A few years later, my aunt (my mom's sister) moved from a neighboring town into a duplex close to my mom. She was older than my mom but in better health. When Mother moved to the other assisted living, her sister, Lena, moved in there as well.

They occupied different apartments on different floors (probably a good thing). By this time, John and I had separated, and I began teaching again in the same school, Southwest Christian School.

My mother's physical and mental health continued to decline. She had endured chronic back pain and arthritic damage for years. Her intense pain sent her to Emergency several times. Each time, the doctors and nurses would medicate her and send her back to her assisted living.

She eventually needed to be on so much medicine for the pain she threw up while sleeping, sucking it into her lungs, and spent her last week of life in intensive care. At the same time, her sister was experiencing her second round of colon cancer and was becoming progressively weaker.

At the time, my daughter, Amy, and her family lived in Louisiana. She lovingly supported me through our conversations on the phone by reassuring me I had what it took to get through this. Albert and I were dating, and he became a tremendous anchor in my storm.

The staff and teachers at Southwest Christian School rallied around me. They substituted for me when I was at the hospital and shared their love and concern over the loss of my mother.

Months after my mom died, my aunt moved to a hospice facility. Albert and I visited her as much as we could, but it saddens me because I was not with her when she died.

Without children, a spouse, or grandchildren, I was responsible for handling her estate and planning her funeral. Her only son died in his forties, and she had buried two husbands and a granddaughter. She had outlived her closest friends. We buried her in Dallas, Texas, which she requested. Albert and I were the only ones there.

Coming Full Circle

Still teaching at Southwest Christian School, Albert helped me settle both of their estates. Once completed, life began to level out a bit. We continued to date after my divorce, and I continued to teach sixth-grade language arts.

Albert and I married in 2010, bought a house in foreclosure in Fort Worth, and began to clean it and make improvements. Once the estates were settled and realizing we had finished our responsibilities, we began contemplating moving to Colorado. I started researching areas and houses online.

We both enjoyed vacationing in Snowmass, Colorado, and when we went there, we would drive to the different towns on the Western Slope to research our options.

After two years, we found a house in Montrose we loved! We bought it in 2012, moved to Colorado, and looked forward to retirement. We settled in, made improvements to our home, made friends, and enjoyed the cooler, drier climate and mountain scenery.

Meeting Dr. Ben Carson

While teaching in Texas, one of the required reading books in sixth grade was *Gifted Hands: The Ben Carson Story* by Dr. Ben Carson. This autobiography shares the life of one of the most celebrated neurosurgeons in the world. In 2016, Ben Carson entered politics and made his bid for the Republican candidacy for President.

In his book, he shares the inspiring journey from his childhood in inner-city Detroit to his position as Director of Pediatric Neurosurgery at Johns Hopkins Hospital at age 33. He is a role model for anyone who aims high and attempts the seemingly impossible. This book highlights the faith and genius that opened the treasures of healing he shared with so many.

He models how passion drives purpose and how they are intertwined. His book motivated my sixth-grade students to have dreams and goals, and not to let circumstances define their success.

It thrilled me to meet him in person in Basalt, Colorado, at a book signing for his book, *America the Beautiful: Rediscovering What Made This Nation Great.* As we visited, I shared with him all the ways his book, *Gifted Hands,* had inspired my sixth graders. Then I explained my retirement from teaching and our move to Colorado.

Dr. Carson listened intently. In his quiet but direct manner, he responded, "But you can't quit working at a job you feel so passionate about." It wasn't so much his words as the look in his eyes as he stared directly into mine that made me slightly uncomfortable. I told Albert what he had said, and I quickly "brushed it off."

Coming full circle, I re-entered the teaching field. I returned to teaching in a public elementary school in Colorado. Dr. Carson was right. **Passion** drives **purpose** and inspires hope.

Writing a Book

Before leaving Fort Worth, my students encouraged me to write a book. I had NO idea what kind of book I would write when I retired, but the challenge intrigued me.

Then in the summer of 2012, after we had moved to Colorado, Albert and I vacationed in Snowmass. We signed up to go horseback riding in the mountains. There were only three of us on the two-hour ride—Albert, the guide, and myself.

Riding behind our guide make it easy for me to visit with this young man about his life. He shared stories about his family and how much he enjoyed meeting people and sharing Colorado with them. I shared my goal of writing a book, and then we stopped talking to enjoy the ride.

Enjoying the quiet peace of the mountain landscape, I started "hearing" ideas for my book! At the end of those two hours, I knew the title, what the book would be about, and even the names of the chapters (treasures).

As soon as we returned to our condominium, I frantically wrote everything exploding from my brain. This book, *Tragedy's Treasures*, would describe twelve treasures that opened for me before, during, and after the death of my son.

I spent six years finishing the manuscript. I have taken many vacations from writing and editing with countless hours spent researching all it takes to publish a book! Do you self-publish or indie-publish? When and how do you market the book? What about the cover, the editing, and the formatting?

I began a website, started blogging to practice my skills, and began developing an email list of loyal readers to give me input and to nudge me toward finishing this book. When I got close to the finish line, I opened the bins of Bart's memorabilia to uncover heart-warming details to include.

My blogging path led me to Laura Cole Gonzalez. Laura is the transformational author of the #1 best-seller *Healthy Business, Healthy You Toolbox* book series, and *Action Attraction Planner* (both available on Amazon) and a Vision Board Coach. She is a marketing mentor for natural health and wellness entrepreneurs and **authors**, which I needed. This **treasure** was NOT an accident!

Laura chose my blog and contacted me to have a complimentary phone consultation with her to help me with my author's journey. Her *Author Solutions System* gave me tools to define my goals and get 'er done!

She "took the reins" of helping me set up my Facebook Author Page and recruiting my Inner Circle of followers to help my book reach #1 on Amazon at launch time!

Since 2016, we have continued to support and learn from each other. I edited Laura's book, *Healthy Business, Healthy You Toolbox*, and she continues to share her technical knowledge about marketing, websites, and social media platforms.

———

My husband, Albert, has been a constant support and encourager in my writing journey. He has frequently asked me questions such as, "What are your goals for...?" "How much further do you have to go on...?" He has repeatedly assured me he believes in me, which has inspired me to keep working and finish what I started!

This book is a mission of love. I have cried, prayed, procrastinated, and started the process over many times. My prayer is for *Tragedy's Treasures* to encourage anyone who reads it to increase their faith in God and His Son and not to give up hope in tragic circumstances.

God is in control, and He loves us enough to help us through ANYTHING! His plan is perfect. It guides us through devastating tragedies and equips us to find hope and joy again.

PART FIVE: THE STORY CONTINUES

"Bad things do happen; how I respond to them defines my character and the quality of my life. I can choose to sit in perpetual sadness, immobilized by the gravity of my loss, or I can choose to rise from the pain and treasure the most precious gift I have - life itself."
—Walter Anderson

MORE TREASURES

"Be joyful in hope, patient in affliction, faithful in prayer."
—Romans 12:12 NIV

December 31, 2015

E ighteen years, two months, and twenty-one days have passed since Bart's accident. Since that horrific day, his loyal friends, their compassionate parents, and many others I don't personally know have shared with me how his death continues to impact and change them.

Christmas Treasures

For at least the first ten years after he died, and always at Christmas, I received an unexpected letter, call, or visit from someone sharing the blessings they experienced because of Bart's life and death.

I wish I had recorded each instance, but one I remember is

when one of Bart's high school friends contacted me and asked to visit with me in person. He came to my classroom after school at Southwest Christian School, and the two of us talked.

I listened in awe as he described how Bart's unconditional friendship and witness stuck with him during high school and into his adult years as he fought his battle with low self-esteem and drug abuse.

He had since invited Christ into his heart and life, stopped using drugs, and wanted me to know Bart's friendship had been a driving force in his life-changing process.

Wow! I had no idea....

We arranged for him to come to the school to give his testimony to 100+ seventh- and eighth-graders during a weekly chapel.

As he told his story, the students, teachers, and visiting parents hung on every word. His story of Bart's influence and God's healing reminded us of the hope and restoration God provides.

Even this Christmas, as I dug the stockings out of the plastic gift-wrap container we store them in, I felt a small bulge in the "Karyn" stocking. I pulled out a note I had received from one of Bart's former teachers. I forgot I had stored it there to reread each Christmas.

Barbara Rothschild was Bart's sixth-grade language arts teacher. Even though she moved away, she still kept in contact with a few of Bart's friends. One of those was Valentina. She shared how in texting with Valentina the night before; she suddenly remembered how Valentina and Bart came to her classroom every day for lunch when they were in seventh grade.

She wrote, "I wanted to let you know I think of Bart often, with incredible fondness. I was so saddened to hear of his death, and had I known, I would have flown in for his funeral. He was a joy to teach, and I always felt so fortunate he wanted to spend his lunchtime with me. Bart, Valentina, and I had many wonderful conversations about so many things!"

She closed her letter by saying, "I am sure this was heart-breaking and devastating. Bart, in his young life, touched many people. Your son is remembered by so many–and after all these years, I wanted to send you my heartfelt condolences."

Valentina now lives in Austin, is married to a wonderful man, and has three adorable girls. I always love getting her sweet letters and messages on Facebook.

I smile as I remember getting a call from Bart when John and I were on a business trip at a tropical resort. Our son asked if we could buy Valentina a bracelet… when he was in the third grade! We soon figured out they were "going together." They continued to be close friends throughout elementary school, middle school, and high school.

I am so grateful to these friends, teachers, and many others who have taken their time to write or contact me to let me know Bart is still remembered and is still making a difference.

Treasured Friends

I doubt most parents get the opportunity to know their children's friends as intimately as I did. In the months following Bart's accident, his friends, teachers, and coaches became a lifeline for me.

When I listened to them talk about Bart, it kept him alive for me and made me feel closer to him. As they told me stories about his personality and "antics," I laughed, cried, and sometimes was even a little embarrassed. But I always appreciated their honesty and love for him. I suspect our talks helped them stay connected to him.

I am thankful to be in contact with many of his closest friends. Though I moved out of Texas, I stayed in touch with Herb Stephens, his golf coach and mentor, until his death in 2019. We became close friends.

I treasure returning to Texas each September to attend the annual Bart Granger Memorial High School golf tournament. This trip gives me the chance to reconnect with coaches and friends who loved Bart.

Mary-Margaret Spikes Lemons was one of his closest friends. She is now a lawyer in Fort Worth, married to Eric, her loving husband, and has two beautiful children. She continues to write me or call me, and I treasure our friendship.

A New Commitment

Adam Rubinson was the number one player on Bart's high school golf team when they won the Paschal Invitational three weeks before his accident.

He was the friend who sat in our living room as John, Amy, and our minister planned Bart's funeral. He sat quietly listening to our beliefs and ideas about death and why we wanted Bart's funeral to be a celebration of his life instead of a morbid, sad service.

In the months and years that followed, Adam came to hear me speak about why I was so sure Bart now lived in heaven with his Creator. I didn't seek out these speaking opportunities; they found me. Adam was always a kind, loving, and a respectful example of the friends who blessed Bart's life.

He still lives in Fort Worth with his beautiful wife and two children. After playing on his college golf team and graduating from Texas Christian University with a business degree, he played professional golf from 2002 to 2009. He then left his job as a pro golfer, married, and started working for Wells Fargo. He is now Vice-President at JM Cox Family Management.

Adam is blessed with a loving family who has supported him and encouraged him to follow his dreams and be the best he can be. His dad is of the Jewish faith, and his mom is a Christ follower. They lovingly allowed Adam and his siblings to follow the path they chose.

After a mutual friend's brother died, Adam sent me this message:

"Thanks for reaching out. I'm glad to see you are writing about Bart and your faith. I wrote the Boyds a note concerning their loss of Bryan last week. I told them I certainly don't understand God's ways ("the mystery of His will"), and I didn't understand why God took Bart, but I do know He used Bart's death to begin my journey toward faith in Christ. HIS ways are unsearchable, but I certainly believe HE works ALL things for the good of those who love HIM.

I hope this is some encouragement for you as you begin this work.

God bless you and your work!"

Adam Rubinson

The Rest of the Story

Then, in 2013[1], Adam wrote the following article for the "Jews for Jesus Online Publication."

"I was born in 1980 to a Jewish father and a mother who was nominally Christian. My father's parents were Orthodox, and my mother's father was Jewish. As a young child, religion was about holidays, and holidays were about family. So, religion was just about family having an excuse to get together and enjoy each other's company and exchange gifts.

We celebrated the Jewish holidays with my dad's family, and the "big one" was the Seder meal. We got together with our family from Dallas. There were, and still are today, about 50-70 of my family members who gather in a hotel in Dallas to eat some stinky fish, look for some crackers in a napkin, and sing some crazy songs at the end. We had to prepare to read the four questions on the way over to Dallas. Why was this night different from all the others? I knew the answers early on. I won the race to find the afikomen about 50 percent of the time, but I never knew why it was hidden in the first place. Also, Elijah never seemed to show up, and that became a joke around the table. "Can't believe he didn't make it this year. Must have been some traffic on I-35."

As I said, my mother was a nominal Christian, so we celebrated Christmas, and Easter with her side of the family.

Christmas was about presents, stockings, Santa and food. The sweet potatoes were great, and we always had stacks of packages to unwrap. Thanksgiving was the same as Christmas, only without the gifts. Easter was about baskets; bunnies, and lots of candy that would end up making my stomach hurt the next day. There was no real meaning to the traditions we were carrying on. We just went through the motions year after year.

During high school, I was a good student and much more of a homebody than most of my friends, but my passion was golf. I kept improving and finished second in the state. Unfortunately, some of my teammates made many derogatory comments about Jews. I would tell them I was a Christian because it was easier than taking grief for being Jewish. One of my teammates (who was not anti-Semitic) was a close friend, and he was killed in an automobile accident. That got me questioning and thinking about eternity.

In 1998, I entered the fall semester as a freshman on the Texas Christian University golf team with dreams for golf, girls, and partying. The funny and fortunate thing for me was that I was terrible at all three. I say "fortunate" because I was preserved from making some really awful decisions. I wasn't cool enough to hang with the golfers. I wasn't cool enough to make friends with the frat guys or sorority girls. I really didn't fit in anywhere. That was a very tough year for me.

The only place I seemed to be able to hang out was at a Bible study hosted by College Golf Fellowship (CGF). Why would I go to a place like that? My impression of Christianity at that point was an old guy with white hair, a brown suit, a yellow shirt, and glasses. Oh yeah, and he was always saying "No." But as I attended this Bible study, I saw Christianity might look boring, but these guys weren't. That got me curious. These guys were Christians, and they still laughed and had fun! That didn't match up with my stereotype at all.

I still wasn't convinced there was any merit to the philosophy or belief system of Christianity. I asked question after question. Most of the time I didn't even wait to hear a response. I either wanted to just be heard, or I was too busy wanting to be my own boss that I rarely even listened for the response. These guys kept loving me and including me when any normal human would have been sick of me and would have stopped inviting me to hang out.

My whole life changed in the spring of 2002. By this time, I had been listening to some of the arguments for Christianity. A pretty strong case was beginning to build, but I still wasn't convinced. Brad Payne with CGF took me to Dallas to hear a man named Dan Korem speak about the Passover, which was coming up. Dan was born into an Orthodox Jewish home and started having questions about Judaism at the age of 18. His parents didn't know how to handle the situation, so they sent him to the rabbi for "fixing". After a long conversation, the rabbi decided Dan needed to become a Christian!

Well, that night in Dallas, Dan went through the Seder meal from his perspective as a Jew who believes in Jesus. He explained dozens of amazing things that foreshadowed Jesus' coming. The Seder foretold of his death and his resurrection. Jesus was the Passover lamb! I understood the hiding of the matzah: middle of the three pieces taken out (Jesus), hidden (buried), found by the children, receive a reward (heaven). That night, I came to believe Jesus was, in fact, the Messiah foretold in the Hebrew Scriptures.

My life has new purpose and a sense of urgency. Urgency, because if at the end of this life, there's either heaven, or hell, it's time to tell the world. However, I've learned to be patient when telling others about Jesus. I recognize God had been preparing me for some time to receive his message. It didn't happen overnight. And while the change was sudden, it took a while to get to that sudden change.

By the way, I did eventually become a pretty good golfer. In 2003 I was chosen as captain of the U.S. Palmer Cup team and I was selected to the U.S. Walker Cup team. These are the highest honors an American amateur golfer can receive. I went on to play on the PGA Tour, the Nationwide Tour, and various mini-tours across the country.

I have recently left the world of professional golf to pursue my role as a husband and father with much more regularity. I live in Fort Worth, Texas, with my wife, Tori, and our two young children, Sami and Ben.

On the journey to becoming a professional golfer, I discovered something more thrilling than the fleeting fame of celebrity and tournaments. That is the fact there is a God who loves me and cares for me, and he wants to be involved in all the details of my life.

My hope for all reading this is for you to take a serious look at Jesus. God loves us enough to have paid our penalty for us. This is all as plain in the Hebrew Scriptures as it is in the New Testament. It's really all one book. If you haven't come to know the Messiah for yourself, please read the Scriptures and consider Jesus' claims. I know for me, a better understanding of my Jewish heritage made it simply natural for me to accept 'the rest of the story.' "

Along with Adam, I firmly believe God does *"work all things for the good..."* (Romans 8:28).

As my minister reminded me after my son died, the Bible doesn't say everything is good... only that God can work devastating tragedies into something good, if we believe. There are too many things in this life we can't explain or understand: suffering, pain, illness, death, disappointment, financial struggles, etc. If only we are willing to ride the wave of grief and hold on tight to hope in the unseen, God can help us trust Him more, praise Him more, and share His love with others.

1   http://www.jewsforjesus.org/publications/blog/rest-of-the-story

Bart Granger

SHARE YOUR STORY

I am sure that many of you reading this book have similar "faith" stories and experiences which could provide comfort and inspire many. Would you please email me and tell me your stories? I promise I won't share them unless I have your permission.

How has tragedy transformed you?

What "treasures" have you opened?

What "gifts" have you received?

I want to hear your thoughts about this book, your experiences, and your questions and comments.

Also, I want to know how I might improve this book.

Email Me:
Kalmendarez@karynalmendarez.com

Connect With Me:
facebook.com/KarynAlmendarezauthor

Join Our **Inner Circle** for news of upcoming books and encouragement:
http://bit.ly/KarynInnerCircle

CAN YOU HELP ME?

Thank You For Reading My Book!

I really appreciate all your feedback, and I love hearing what you have to say.

Reviews are gold to authors! If you've enjoyed this book, would you consider rating and reviewing it on Amazon?
Click **Here**

https://openyourtreasures.com/reviews/

Thanks again for your support!

To thank you for reading, I would like to give you a free gift, and keep you up to date with new releases and special offers.

Get Your Copy **HERE**

https://openyourtreasures.com/free-gift-self-care-journal/

ABOUT THE AUTHOR

Karyn Almendarez is a retired school teacher, writer, and free-lance proofreader.

She wrote this book to comfort and encourage grieving parents (or anyone who has lost a loved one) to travel through their grief journey with patience, self-care, and hope. She lives in Colorado with her husband, Albert. She is also a breast cancer thriver who enjoys clean eating, hiking, and snow skiing.

Go here to learn more and connect with her:

https://openyourtreasures.com/learn-more-about-karyn/

ENDNOTES

Treasure #2: Called to Mother

1. http://www.drfoot.co.uk/wrist_pain/Kienbocks.html
2. "About." *Young Life.* N.p., n.d. Web. 29 June 2016.

Treasure #5: Called to Trust

1. *"The Courage of Conviction." Our Daily Bread.* N.p., Web. *29 June 2016*

Treasure #8: Gift of Remembering

1. "High School Golf Scoreboard." *12th Annual Bart Granger Memorial Golf Tournament to Be Played September 18th-19th 2009 -.* N.p., n.d. Web. 29 June 2016.

Treasure #11: Gift of Sharing

1. "EPublications." *Organ Donation and Transplantation Fact Sheet.* N.p., n.d. Web. 29 June 2016.